"Dr. Fos...d save not only your life ...*...e Song* is a message of lov...*...*...*...*...* its author to all who read his stories. Like some of the best nature writers we have known; Thoreau, Emerson, Muir, and Leopold, this book is an inspiration for those longing to connect with nature, the soul, and a love for all creation. It is a powerful road map and compass for all of us who long for the hope of a new creation. It guides us toward finding our way home to our divine nature. I highly recommend this book."

— Dr. Steve Poos-Benson, Speaker, Pastor
Author, *Sent to Soar: Fulfill Your Divine
Potential for Yourself and the World*

"I've known Foster Harding for decades and am excited that he has written *Creation Is a Love Song* to share his life experiences, wisdom, and high consciousness. This book is a powerful and unique intersection of ecology and spirituality. I especially appreciate the laser-focused "Love and wisdom" offered for direct application to the readers' life. Foster's work is imperative for all who seek to see our universe through the lens of Oneness, where all sentient beings are connected. All of us, from activists to those who are feeling helpless, can benefit from his numinous writing."

— Rev. Dr. David Goldberg, Interim Pastor, Unity of Denver
and former Publisher at Centers for Spiritual Living.

"*Creation Is a Love Song* is well written and very inspiring. It reminds us that we are all connected to land and nature. It is a wonderful story about Foster Harding's feelings and emotions based on his experiences growing up on the land and in the midst of nature, and through his travels. Throughout his life he continues to be drawn to what Mother Earth provides. His writing helps us understand that land and nature are part of all of us, and we, as humans, need to appreciate and protect what Mother Earth provides in order to grow and thrive during our lifetime, and allow future generations to do the same."

— Patti Hostetler, Executive Director,
Douglas Land Conservancy

"*Creation Is a Love Song* is a magnificent voyage. Travel with Foster to intriguing locations all over our Earth, and into unseen realms of the Universe. Foster is skilled at bringing the reader into the heart of his experiences, creating vivid and visceral encounters with nature, and imparting deep wisdom gleaned from living nearly 80 years on this planet. This book will feed any mind intent on forging a deeper connection with nature and within themselves."

— AnnaBeth Davidson,
editor of *Creation Is a Love Song*

FOSTER LAVERNE HARDING

CREATION IS A LOVE SONG

Foreword by Dr. Steve Poos-Benson

Creation is a Love Song
Published by FosMar Books
Castle Rock, CO

ISBN: 978-0-578-34242-9
BODY, MIND & SPIRIT / Inspiration & Personal Growth

Cover by Barbara Lane and Interior design by Victoria Wolf.
Copyright owned by Foster Laverne Harding.

QUANTITY PURCHASES: Schools, companies, professional
groups, clubs, and other organizations may qualify for special terms
when ordering quantities of this title. For information, email
fosharding@msn.com.

"The message of *Creation Is a Love Song* is critical for all of us to hear, understand, and integrate into our lives. It's author's deep reflection on the key issues of our time comes across on every page."

— Tim Rouse, Co-founder, Futures Group Int'l (FGI)

"*Creation Is a Love Song* merges history, science, and mysticism in this collection of essays about the author's life experiences. It speaks to your inner poet and intensifies your thirst for greater connection with yourself and all life. Foster's stories read like love songs. His stories open your heart and inspire you to notice the love songs in your own life. As I finished the last page, I felt expanded by the magnificence of God in all life."

— Paige Farrington Prendergast,
Founder of Love ➙ Ignites ➙ Peace

"When I despair, I remember that all through history the ways of truth and love have always won ... think of it — always."
— John Briley, from the screenplay for *Gandhi*

"It is fear that binds and limits a soul; it is love that frees and cuts away all bonds."
— Eileen Caddy, *Opening Doors Within*

"Love is an experience of infinity."
— Yogi tea tag quote

Also by Foster Laverne Harding:

The Great University of Life: A Soul Journey Progress Report, Park Point Press, Golden, Colorado (2013)

Creation Is a Love Song is dedicated to all who do their best to live in love and gratitude. Thank you for leading the way.

The foundation for this book is anchored here:

Love Song – The Child
As a child I heard
notes of beauty
amid bird song
and wind music.
A love song came;
mine to sing,
so daunting it seemed
an error — or a dream.
Why does my song
feel so far beyond me?

— FLH

Creation is an eternal love song. Each of us is a singer.
Singers come and go every day, but the song lives on.
When I allow the song to sing me, I become one with the sacred.
Then there is only the song.

— FLH

Contents

Guest Foreword

It was a brilliant early June evening in Yellowstone. My wife and I were on the lookout for wolves along the road that winds through the Lamar Valley. It was dusk and a chill had settled in the valley as we stopped at a pull-out to use my spotting scope. There he was, a smoky black male on top of a ridge. He stood tall; his head laid back in a long howl. Was he calling to his mate or the rest of the pack? Standing in his presence, the lone wolf touched a deep part of me I can only describe as my soul. It felt like he was calling me.

I have had other encounters in the natural world that struck a deep chord like that evening in Yellowstone. In the midst of a snowstorm, I came upon a large mountain lion slinking cross the road. One summer I assisted a bear biologist in Alaska tagging and transporting grizzlies. As I held open the mouth of a tranquilized grizzly so her teeth could be examined, her eyes locked onto mine, rattling my senses and filling me with awe. Out hiking one autumn at sundown, a bull elk bellowed from the dark timber and then stepped out. He held his six-point rack like a sentinel as he again bugled, his breath billowing a cloud in the gathering dusk.

In each instance something was sparked inside of me. There was a divine longing; a depth of being was touched that awakened in me a mystical awareness of the vast primordial void. From these encounters I've learned that my soul sings when it's in the midst of the natural world. There is something from nature that awakens me out of my daily existence and takes me to a place that feels like home.

I am not alone. Countless thousands of people feel a similar depth of being that comes to them from nature. Whether it's a trek through Nepal, a backpack through the Sierras, or watching the birds at your feeder in the backyard, our souls yearn for what the wild can bring.

The wild in nature stimulates the wild inside of us to step beyond routine daily existence and see our lives as a wild expression of the spinning Cosmos.

Sometimes the freedom can be so stunning and inspiring, it can lead beyond exhilaration into fear. Nature can be so disarming and alarming that we need those who have ventured into the unknown wild and come back to show us the way forward. These people are more than nature lovers; they are like shamans of the spiritual journey who are able to see beyond this world into the next. They take us by the hand and lead us forward as we venture into the wild of the Cosmos.

Dr. Foster Harding is my spiritual shaman. Foster and I have known each other for over thirty years. We have taught classes and enjoyed meals together. We have even led a memorial service for a mutual friend who had died.

What I love about Foster is that he never stops exploring the frontiers of the spiritual life. He is always coming back and guiding those of us who are yearning for more, but are not quite sure to how go forward. I will never forget when Foster unlocked the mysteries of the soul for me. He helped me see that our souls are not limited to just one lifetime, but are part of a journey that ventures through hundreds, if not thousands of lifetimes. Foster's concept of the wild as it relates to the soul, exploded my concepts and opened me up to the possibility that I have been here many previous lifetimes and have more to come. Conversations with Foster are like taking the hand of a wise shaman who has explored the depths of existence and is now going to take you beyond where you are and what you know.

When I first read *Creation Is a Love Song*, I felt the wild shaman speaking to me yet again. As Foster explains the natural world through his treks, hikes, and working in his garden, he takes the wild and surrounds it with a vocabulary that, for the willing voyager, acts as a guiding map. Through his own experience he points, explains, and encourages the willing adventurer to embrace their journey into the wild of their soul.

Creation Is a Love Song inspired me as Foster described that this wild ride is actually the way the Cosmos wraps us with love. That which we might fear is how the God or Goddess tenderly cares for our lives and touches our soul. The wild is not something to be feared but to follow as it reveals a soul map that leads us back to our own natural home.

One day over lunch I laid out on the table some of the things I was wrestling with in my spiritual life. The wise shaman looked at me and instead of providing ready answers he simply said, "Let your soul be your guide." It was as if he put the hiker's staff into my hand and said, "Venture forth! Get in touch with the depth of your being and allow it to lead you forward. Trust nature, trust the wild, trust your soul, it will lead you where you need to go."

One of the lines from *Creation Is a Love Song* rang my inner bell. Foster says, "Your soul will always lead you home." If we're willing to get in touch with the wild inside, awaken to the sacred, and listen to that which has been traveling with us for millennia, it will always take us to a place we can trust. It will always bring us back to safety. It will wrap us in love. It will take us home.

Foster has been on the planet for a while. I think he said in *The Great University of Life* that his soul has cycled over four hundred times. During this soul adventure he's learned a lot and he's always willing to share. If you can't find him to have a cup of coffee or enjoy lunch, read this book. Let the shaman open up your world, let him point you to love. Let him put the staff in your hand and hear him say, "Go forward. Go to the wild. Go home."

Dr. Steve Poos-Benson, Speaker, Pastor
Author of *Sent to Soar: Fulfill Your Divine Potential for Yourself and the World*

Introduction

In this book, I have done my best to honor any expectations my friend Steve's foreword may have generated. The main title, *Creation Is a Love Song*, reflects my deep conviction that the divine energy of creation eternally sings the Universe and its myriad expressions into existence. The Bible says, "In the beginning was the word ..." but my heart knows that creation continually arises within God as a song of love and joy. Here on Earth, I feel a Divine Mother singing her beloved planet into being with a lullaby. For me, creation *is* a love song that includes everything with no exceptions. The subtitle *Heaven on Earth Is Within Your Reach*, evolved with the book. It changed as often as a debutant adjusts hair and makeup before her first ball.

Creation Is a Love Song is a mirror reflecting its author's evolution from a young child to an elder called to share his love and wisdom with the world. My journey from childhood to elderhood has been a tumultuous trek. The book shows that we can see and engage the opportunities buried within our tangled myriad of problems. My intention is to give hope and inspiration to a world filled with turmoil and desperation. The work required to co-create heaven on earth belongs to all of us. Let's go for a walk.

Something is Calling

"Let yourself be silently drawn by the strange pull of what you really love. It will not lead you astray."
— Rumi

"But especially he loved to run in the dim twilight of the summer midnights, listening to the subdued and sleepy murmurs of the forest, reading signs and sounds as a man may read a book, and seeking for the mysterious something that called — called, waking or sleeping, at all times, for him to come."
— Jack London, *The Call of the Wild*

Since birth, an inner longing has been calling me toward an expanded sense of freedom. In my latter seventies, I have finally learned that freedom comes from living in harmony with my true self. For much of my life, I was oblivious to the idea of a true self, and was naïve enough to seek freedom in the world outside myself. *Creation Is a Love Song* shows how my relationship with Nature opened the door to a pathway that has finally led me home.

Nature has been my life-long refuge from low self-esteem, the pressures of being bullied as a kid, and the stresses of college, career, and retirement. It is an uncompromising context, doing nothing to take care of an inexperienced boy exploring alone. I gradually learned to take care of myself, and expand my explorations as my capacities grew. So, despite the unforgiving ways of nature, I came to feel unfettered in the wild — more aware and alive. Nature provides a sense of belonging, with space to learn about myself and commune with a much more loving God than formal religion ever provided. This Beloved is an inner presence closer than my own breath. A lifetime of wilderness experiences with dangerous weather, getting lost, fatigue, and wild creatures brought fear on many occasions. Yet, the Beloved has always been with me and I have always been okay. I gradually learned not to be afraid in the wild. Nature taught me that seeking my true self and searching for God are the same quest.

Early retirement offered fresh opportunity to respond to the call for expanded freedom. After decades, the quest gradually shifted from *where* I am to *who* I am — from trying to create perfect external circumstances to exploring my inner landscapes. Lately, the call feels like authenticity and wholeness calling me home to myself. I must be my authentic self before I can *feel* whole. The second half of life has brought gradual realization that I came into this life to *be* love. All my soul's many incarnations have been preparation for that recognition. When I accept my innate wholeness, that long-sought freedom is naturally present. Inner freedom is delicious, but I need not fear the deep slumber of a satisfied mind.

Love is still calling me deeper into its infinite wholeness. May it always be so.

Heaven on Earth is Within Our Reach

Most world citizens who read the above title might conclude its author is either delusional, or the most naïve senior citizen on the planet. I am neither crazy nor naïve. My own life experiences have taught me that *heaven on earth* is within our reach. Notice, I did not say it is already in our grasp. There is much change to be embraced before we shift from where we are, to where we'd like to be. But it is, for each of us, within the reach of our potential to actually co-create a shift in our experience of daily life, to include more and more heaven on earth. I am experiencing the unfolding of this shift daily, so I am confident when I say it is within our reach. Believe me, I was not born with an excess of potential; if it can come to me, life can shift for you, or any dedicated seeker.

Having said that, I do not see heaven on earth as a goal with a specific destination and timeframe. Indeed, heaven on earth may mean something quite different to every person who considers the phrase. For me, it is *being* love, which is accompanied by a deep sense of well-being and abundance anchored in trusting God and life. Life is demonstrating every day that I have everything I need, *as I need it.* Our fears and urges to plan, save, and hoard are simply a sign to remind us we are all a work in progress, having not yet reached complete trust in God and life. I trust that all of humanity and Mother Earth's problems, from COVID-19, to unrest from economic and social inequities, to global climate change, along with whatever problems you may want to add, can be shifted toward heaven on earth. All our problems lie within reach of our collective capacity to change.

Like life itself, moving toward heaven on earth is a process. Our experiences of life in the outer world almost perfectly reflect our inner life landscapes. Whether our beliefs and attitudes lift us up or depress us, they effectively frame and shape our response to outer conditions, and thus, our experience of the world. If we believe we are victims of life's cruel twists, outer conditions will reflect challenging life experiences, and we will become ever more isolated from heaven on earth. On the other hand, if we trust God and life, our experience of life moves toward heaven on earth. Human beings are, by nature, creatures with free will and choice. It is our job, as individuals, to accept what is ours to do.

I see the extraordinary challenges of these tumultuous times as the reflection into the world around us, of all our collective inner fears, beliefs, and attitudes. My own life has taught me that once you commit, deep within yourself, to move toward heaven on earth, God and life will provide opportunities for you. All you have to do is say "yes." Experiencing heaven on earth is, first and foremost, *inner* work. As a person moves into the flow of that process, it becomes clearer what is theirs to do in service to the outer world. Positive shifts flow most effectively from the inside out.

Creation Is a Love Song shares how the flow of life taught me that I am a being of love, who experiences heaven on earth every day for much of the time. Life isn't perfect nirvana just yet, but the arc of its unfolding is clear. It is my intent and hope that the book provides love, wisdom, and guidance to help you engage, with trust and confidence, your own pathway toward heaven on earth. Your inner growth and work in the world are important, but striving and struggle are *not* required. Please remember that you are loved by God and are allowed to trust life and enjoy your journey. May peace and joy accompany you.

The Glade of Awakening

After wandering inner and outer wildernesses in search of *something* for almost eighty years, there is a growing sense of finally approaching a place where meaning feels close. This morning I found myself in a sacred dreamscape; a glade deep in a primeval forest temple. The soft, warm light carried gratitude for new clarity about humanity and our place in creation. It was deeply peaceful to be there.

All humanity has been wandering for endless millennia through the wilderness of daily life, absorbed by its drama of urgencies and priorities. Only a relative few have sensed the possibility that life could hold meaning beyond survival. So, the glade where awareness took me this morning felt remarkably spacious, almost lonely, like I might be the only one around. But divine love is everywhere, so I am never truly alone.

There is a long history of people, from ancient avatars and prophets to more recent seekers, seers, and sages, who found their own glade of awakening. Within my own experience, two spiritual eco-village communities have emerged to showcase a thriving way of life in harmony with Mother Earth. The founders of Findhorn (in Scotland) and Damanhur (in Italy) were surely anchored in, and co-created from, such a glade of awakening. These, and other spiritual eco-villages around the globe, have coalesced around love-centered wisdom to shine the power of divine love. These are places where the sacred and the temporal merge into a thriving relationship with Mother Earth and all life. Indeed, they are a love offering to the world that demonstrates heaven on earth actually unfolding here and now. Such examples await humanity's wider recognition and embrace.

Applied Kinesiology

While each soul does its best to inspire and guide the life of its human host, life has taught me to be wary of my ego as I try to discern my pathway. So, I was relieved and delighted to discover David Hawkins' teachings about applied kinesiology twenty years ago. Since then, those teachings have remarkably supported my spiritual growth.

To avoid confusion when discussing Dr. Hawkins' use of kinesiology, it is important to recognize that different uses have evolved in the practice of kinesiology since the 1850's. Kinesiology originally was limited to the scientific study of human or non-human body movement, which focused on biomechanics, and is applied in fields such as orthopedics, sports medicine, and physical therapies. The term kinesiology, coming from Greek language, basically translates as "movement science." The practice was developed in Stockholm, Sweden in 1854, by Professor Carl August Georgii.[i]

Applied kinesiology evolved from the original practice. The International College of Applied Kinesiology (founded in 1976) states, "The combined terms 'applied' and 'kinesiology' describe the basis of this system, which is the use of manual muscle testing to evaluate body function through the dynamics of the musculoskeletal system."[ii] Applied Kinesiology, as used by various practitioners, examines the chemical, structural, and mental aspects of an individual through the use of muscle testing.

David R. Hawkins' work combines the practices of applied kinesiology and behavioral kinesiology (now called Life-Energy Analysis), which was pioneered by Dr. John Diamond in the late 1970's. Throughout this book, I will be referring to the use of applied kinesiology, as described by David R Hawkins, MD, PhD.[iii]

In the last third of the twentieth century, Dr. Hawkins was a medical doctor with a large clinical practice in New York City, which was world-renowned for miraculous healings. At the height of his career, a serious illness nearly claimed his life. That near-death experience changed everything for Dr. Hawkins. He closed his practice, moved to Sedona, Arizona, and began a life of spiritual service to the world. Hawkins discovered an amazing extension of applied kinesiology, claiming that the body has the capacity to tell truth from falsehood. Since studying his work, I have learned to use applied kinesiology to bring clarity to inspiration and guidance.

It helps me discern ego mind chatter from my inner soul voice so I understand what to act upon and what to set aside.

Rather than think of applied kinesiology as a mysterious innate function of the body, I have come to see it as a process through which my soul communicates via muscle responses to guide me through life. Then I don't have to figure out how the body knows truth from falsehood. I already believe my soul knows the answers I need.

I won't duplicate Dr. Hawkins' detailed descriptions of applied kinesiology and how to reliably use his technique, since he covers that brilliantly in his book, *Power vs. Force.*[iv] It is critical to work with a genuinely curious and detached mindset. If you care deeply about the outcome, or believe you already know the answer, your internal bias can sway the applied kinesiology response to align with your anticipated result. One can easily fool themselves if not careful, so I urge caution for those who work with applied kinesiology.

When all is said and done, applied kinesiology has become a trusted tool to discern the pathway my soul is guiding me to walk. I have used applied kinesiology to confirm that the content of this book is in harmony with my soul and speaks spiritual truth. My resulting trust in the book's integrity is a blessing for both me, the author, and I hope, for the reader.

Kissing Mother Earth

"Walk as if you are kissing the Earth with your feet."
— Thich Nhat Hanh, *Peace is Every Step*

"Science without religion is lame, religion without science is blind."
— Albert Einstein, *Science and Religion*

One purpose for *Creation Is a Love Song* is to awaken love for Mother Earth in the hearts of readers. To paraphrase Thich Nhat Hanh, this book called me to write as if I am kissing Mother Earth with my words.

While technology surely provides an important set of tools for the path forward, it can only go so far in healing the pain and suffering we have brought to Mother Earth, each other, and all life. As Einstein implies above, technology and love need each other. Love has the power to heal pain, suffering, and relationships in ways technology cannot touch. Shifting the foundation for the human brain's operating system from fear to love can open the door to heaven on earth. In truth, I don't think there is another way for humanity to reach that state. Humanity has already embraced technology. In order for technology to be married with love before it is too late, we must move toward *being* love. Today is the perfect time to begin our preparations for the wedding of technology and love.

Mother Earth's natural systems are remarkably resilient; she knows how to heal herself far better than we could ever manage. So, humanity does not have to pull off a miracle to heal her directly.

What we must heal are our relationships with Mother Earth and each other. We must shift our attitudes of domination over nature and competition with each other to an attitude of loving cooperation. We must stop wrecking the natural systems that have sustained life on Earth for eons. In some cases, we also must take action to correct the damage we have caused. The major shift in our relationships with Mother Earth, each other, and all life must happen *within us*. Mother Earth can heal herself once we make the choice to love and respect her.

It feels miraculous that *Creation Is a Love Song* arrived in the world at all. I was stuck from the beginning because I just wasn't ready. The vastness of creation meant no book could do more than skim its edges. How could one express a love as vast as nature? My efforts to create the book would never have borne fruit without inspiration from deep within my being. Meditation was essential to set my ego-driven striving aside. What the book would say was revealed as it was written. It became far more than my initial vision because it arrived by flowing *through* me. Writing *Creation Is a Love Song* taught me that inspiration is a matter of allowing; the book flowed of its own volition when I was sufficiently open and trusting. Life experience has brought the realization that the book is an expression of my soul.

CHAPTER 1
SEARCHING FOR WISDOM

"This we know. The Earth does not belong to us; we belong to the Earth. All things are connected, like the blood that unites one family. Whatever befalls the Earth, befalls the children of the Earth. We do not weave the web of life; we are only a strand of it. Whatever we do to the web, we do to ourselves."
— Ted Perry, for the film *Home* [1]

Whether we look at humanity's origins or our personal birth, the context for human life has always been the natural world of Planet Earth. Because Homo sapiens evolved in harmony with Mother Earth, our body appetites and rhythms still belong to her. This remains true despite the illusion of isolation from

---

1   Some readers may be familiar with this quote as being attributed to Chief Seattle. However, this particular statement was written for the television script for the movie, *Home,* by Ted Perry, and cannot be directly attributed to any of the translations of the speeches or words directly credited to Chief Seattle.

nature for many who live in cities and suburbs. For those who seek a relationship with nature, she is all around us, even in city centers where parks, trees, flowers, rooftop gardens, and aviaries are nature in action. All life everywhere is nature expressing herself; even dandelions growing through sidewalk cracks and ants bustling about making the crack a home.

I was blessed to grow up in a small town surrounded by family farms with streams, fields, and wooded areas. I loved wandering the fields and forests of my youth; it was exciting, and as natural as breathing, to explore and learn from nature almost every day. I have never outgrown the sense of wonder in the outdoors I knew as a child. My life has retained that youthful love story with the natural world despite the complexities and responsibilities of adulthood. Education, career, two marriages, and family have all had to make room for my relationship with nature. When I am *out there,* the urgency of everything else fades into balance and I come home refreshed. I have come to see that my love of nature is a reflection of God's love for all creation.

Chapter 1 is rooted in my heart's resonance with today's American Indians. My longing to find common ground is energized by empathy for the suffering they have endured, along with my admiration for the deep Earth wisdom embodied in their daily lives and indigenous worldview. I also write about them because, of all our nation's minority people, they seem to be most absent from our greater awareness in the twenty-first century. The gap in trust between American Indians and Euro-Americans[2] is wide, so I have yet to experience a relaxed friendship with an American Indian. I am willing and hopeful for that during this lifetime.

In writing this chapter, I wanted to be sensitive and use terms that were comfortable for the Indians who still know the Americas as home. There were once many hundreds of groups of indigenous people scattered across the Americas. Each was distinct in their own minds from the others, even though they held in common similar origin stories and respect/reverence for Mother Earth. Because they knew themselves to be distinct groups, it was challenging to find a language umbrella to collectively encompass the people who originally lived throughout the Americas. In the gnarly realm of legal treaties and other legal proceedings, the U.S. government often referred to them by tribal names. By mid-twentieth century, various legislative or bureaucratic actions referring to the aggregate indigenous population seemed to settle on the term *Native Americans*. Because of where this term originated, some American Indians resent it, while others think it's okay. Although its use is common, I've chosen not to use it. Tribal names are used where it makes sense; otherwise, *American Indians* is used most often.

---

2   "Euro-American" is a term coined by Joseph M. Marshall III, a wise and gifted Lakota author of several books about his people's traditions and way of life.

Ancient Wisdom in the Twenty-First Century

"Creation is the first Bible ... and it existed for 13.7 billion years before the second Bible was written. Natural things like animals, plants, rocks, and clouds give glory to God just by being themselves, just what God intended them to be. It is only we humans who have been given the free will to choose not to be what God created us to be."
— Richard Rohr, *Daily Meditation 5/22/20*

I still remember what I felt as a five-year-old looking out across the schoolyard through our upstairs hall window at the forested hills behind our house. It must have been summer because the hills were a symphony of greens, from the light shades of birch leaves dancing in the sun to the dark pine needles whispering in the breeze. I felt a deep yearning to wander those wooded hills cascading in layers to the horizon. They were pulling at my heart strings like magnetism to come and explore, play, grow, and discover. I had no way to know at the time, but the woods were calling me to begin a new song; my song.

Today's awareness began to open as I was looking through that same upstairs window. As a child the sensations were simpler than my understanding now. Back then, I just felt a strong urge to go there. It turned out to be the dawn of a love relationship with nature that has been with me ever since. Today, the love that spoke to my heart as a child, saturates my bones and fills my being. Much of it found its way inside while in the natural world. All the words I have cannot express the gratitude I feel.

After reading two books by Michael Newton (*Journey of Souls* and *Destiny of Souls)* I have come to believe each of us came into this life to find joy and engage lessons chosen by our soul before it merged with our fetus in the womb of our birth mother.[v] Today, it is easy to see that my lifelong love of wild nature is a cornerstone upon which my entire life has rested. Of course, as a child I knew nothing of that — I just wanted to go outside. My soul knew I would need to start building that relationship early.

Over the next seventy years, my view of creation and who I am has expanded to embrace the Cosmos as family. My heart leaps with joy when I look at NASA pictures of the Universe; my soul's home is a place like that. If we were astronauts and could view Earth from a great distance, we would see that our cosmic neighborhood *is* a place like that. Without that oneness with nature, I would not be who I am.

When anthropologists peel back the layers of history to study human cultures and their origins, it seems likely that humanity's first ideas about gods and religion arose within small clans of hunter-gatherers. In our early days, wild nature was the only context for daily life. So, life centered around avoiding predators and securing food, water, and shelter. The beginnings of humanity's spiritual awareness arose within this natural world.

Looking back to the early days of Christianity, and even before, Franciscan priest Richard Rohr has referred to nature as the first revelation of God.[vi] He boldly suggests that early nature-based religions were in some ways more in harmony with the teachings of Jesus than the modern church. The second paragraph in the following essay, *Avatars*, explains how I believe this came about. Just because a belief system is ancient, does not mean it is irrelevant!

Avatars

"If it seems too good to be true, it probably is."
— old adage

A handful of avatars have been scattered like jewels across human history. They wandered amongst the people and places of their time, sharing their love and wisdom by word and example. Their focus was often to eliminate human suffering, because it was so prevalent. They taught the importance of love in human relationships and our relationship with the Divine. In the presence of an avatar, people felt spiritual power to such a degree that spontaneous healings were frequent. The loving wisdom of an avatar also added depth to their teachings beyond what their words alone could carry.

When a great spiritual teacher completes their earthly sojourn, the vibrant power of their teachings tends to fade into something ordinary humans can more easily grasp. Even if perfect records were available of their every word and act, human understanding of their teachings would still dissipate to a fraction of the love and wisdom they carried. Once an avatar leaves the earth plane, their life can become legendary, even as the adage above comes into play. In Jesus' case, three-plus centuries after his death, Christianity became the official religion of the Roman Empire (The Roman Catholic Church). The New Testament passages where Jesus spent many days out in nature finding inner sustenance and strength were ignored to minimize a key part of the pagan religions they intended to replace. Instead, people were taught that their only access to God was through the church. Nature, where Jesus himself found connection with God, had been officially set aside. I believe separating nature from Christianity is why many people struggle to accept ancient stories of miraculous healings or teachings that seem *too good to be true*. Sadly, for many in the twenty-first century, an avatar's life seems like a fairy tale no longer real or connected to modern life. Looking to an avatar for guidance can feel like sorting through ancient scriptures distorted across centuries of cultural differences, and diluted by too many translations, manipulations, and misinterpretations. One wonders how closely what one is reading compares with the avatar's intent, and whether the scriptures are even relevant after so many centuries.

Perhaps a more effective way to find divine inspiration and guidance is to look where the avatars looked. They all pointed to a source of love and wisdom *within* their own being. Love and wisdom flowed into their lives via an inner connection with Divinity itself. Avatars did *not* seek to teach us they were gods, nor did they desire that we seek our answers from them. They came to show us how to live and find our own answers by looking within our own being. They knew that *every* human being is blessed with an inner spring of love and wisdom. They used and recommended prayer, meditation, and contemplation because those tools help us connect with our inner source. Like the avatars, the guidance and inspiration we seek await discovery within our own being.

A Sad Legacy

Indigenous cultures across the globe predate or were isolated from the avatars of recorded history. Yet their remnant populations scattered around today's world seem to innately embody similar wisdom, often via their connections with the realms of nature. Whether or not it is intended, modern society exerts enormous pressure on these ancient cultures. Their simple way of living attuned to nature's rhythms looks like struggle and deprivation to many people. Some feel sorry for indigenous people and want to help them; relatively few seek to understand and learn from them. Others covet their remaining remnants of land and resources with little regard for the indigenous people they'd like to brush aside. In any case, the ancient ones' cultures are precarious. Yet, they have much to teach us. They are children of God as much as the rest of us, often with unique windows upon the Divine. How can we not, at the very least, honor their humanity and allow them the freedom to be who they are? The following essays highlight the consistently dismal Euro-American record in that regard.

Beginning shortly after Columbus' discovery of the Americas, colonization began. Exploitation, extermination, and disease drastically reduced the numbers of American Indians; it is difficult to document the disaster, but estimates of death run as high as ninety percent. Intentional or not, this cleared the path for Euro-American expansion. Our Euro-American ancestors also kidnapped millions of Africans, whom they chose to view as less than fully human, and sold them into slavery in the Americas over the next three-plus centuries.[vii] These behaviors are so out of step with our favored Euro-American *story* about US history! We have always wanted to see ourselves as a nation that welcomes immigrants with open arms. Yet, with the exception of slavery, the openness of our borders has always had a strong bias in favor of white Europeans. Even into the twenty-first century, people of color have consistently had more immigration issues than other groups of society. Even though our policies favored white Europeans, each wave of new immigrants were relegated to the bottom rungs of society's ladder. A detached observer might conclude we were taking advantage of miserable conditions elsewhere in the world to import cheap labor for our economic and industrial growth. For the entire history of the New World, our leaders have often given the economy priority over human dignity and safety.

My observation, after reading Howard Zinn's book, *A People's History of the United States*, is that, from their beginning, governments around the world, from democratic to totalitarian, have always tended to favor and protect those who hold power and wealth, and the processes that brought it to them. So far as I can see, it is human nature for those who reach the top to do their best to protect their position, or, when that becomes no longer feasible, try to pass their power on to their political or family heirs.

Crazy Horse

"Crazy Horse dreamed and went into the world where there is nothing but the spirits of all things ... He was on his horse in that world, and the horse and himself on it and the trees and the grass and the stones and everything were made of spirit, and nothing was hard, and everything seemed to float ... It was this vision that gave him his great power, for when he went into a fight, he had only to think of that world to be in it again, so that he could go through anything and not be hurt ... I think it was only the power of his great vision that made him great."
— John G. Neihardt, *Black Elk Speaks*

While in his mid-teens, Crazy Horse was already well on his way to becoming a warrior. The vision Black Elk refers to likely happened while he was away by himself for a few days in preparation to be a warrior. His Lakota descendants hold his memory in reverence because of his selfless leadership and his remarkable success as a warrior. He was never defeated in his twenty-two battles with rival tribes or the US Cavalry. Crazy Horse was a key strategist in the American Indians' stunning victory over Custer's Cavalry at Little Big Horn. He was completely dedicated to his people and relentless in defending their right to live in freedom on their ancestral lands. In the tumultuous times of our nation's westward expansion, he and his band of Oglala were the last group to be starved into submission by the Army and buffalo hide hunters. His adamant refusal to relinquish their freedom is on a par with any great leader in the history of our nation.

But even Crazy Horse could not resist when the buffalo were slaughtered beyond any hope of sustaining his people. Their resistance was undone when there was no food and no place to find it. So, he was persuaded to come into Fort Robinson, in present-day northwest Nebraska, by other Lakota chiefs who had already surrendered the fate of their people to the US Government. The military commanders at Fort Robinson had made many promises, sometimes with sincere intentions, which were not supported by Congress, their military superiors, or the corrupt logistics system that was supposed to deliver supplies to the Indians.

When Crazy Horse finally came in from his camp on Beaver Creek, his purpose was to negotiate conditions for his people to join reservation life. The Army saw it as their opportunity to arrest him. When Crazy Horse was being taken to a guard house at Fort Robinson, its barred windows revealed their trap. He tried to escape, but in the resulting melee, he was fatally bayoneted in the back by one of the soldiers and died in a few minutes.[viii] The last great war leader of the plains Indians was thus spared heart-wrenching confinement on September 5, 1877. Crazy Horse was only thirty-three.[3]

The vibrant current of indigenous freedom finally went dormant when the Oglala were sent to the Pine Ridge Reservation.

---

3   This short summary of Crazy Horse's life is a very truncated version of private oral and written information. My intention is to protect the right of the Oglala people to decide who shares their history, and respect the person who shared it with me.

The American Indian was finally sequestered — it took three hundred eighty-five years from Columbus' first arrival. We are left to ponder Crazy Horse, his powerful vision, leadership, and love of freedom. Our nation still has no idea what was lost as we finally won this long-sought *victory*. Even now, we don't have the wisdom to see that our own freedom is immeasurably diminished every time we deny it to another.

Crazy Horse's legacy is as compelling for today's Lakota as it was in the 19th century. In early summer of 2015, we joined some friends at Fort Robinson State Park in northwest Nebraska to observe and support the Lakota from the Pine Ridge Reservation as they undertook the 18th annual Crazy Horse Ride. On a Saturday afternoon two hundred Lakota and their horses gathered at Fort Robinson. It was orderly in a self-assembled way; no-one seemed to be in charge, yet everyone knew what to do. The ride would cover the hundred miles from Fort Robinson back to their reservation in South Dakota. On Sunday morning over a hundred riders assembled on the parade ground in front of the marker noting that Crazy Horse had died on this spot. The three lead riders each carried a Lakota staff, one decorated with eagle feathers, one held an American flag, and the last a black MIA flag. We were told that in past years the whole procession had been led by a riderless horse to symbolize fallen military warriors. The horse had always known the way home to Pine Ridge, but this year there was no such horse to lead the ride.

The Lakota organizer of this event since its first year, took great pains to make clear that the ride was to honor our veterans, and that it was open to anyone who wanted to come. In fact, a handful of visitors from the US, Australia, Germany, and a couple of other European nations rode that year. Honoring our veterans is indeed an important point for the Lakota, since many of them join the US military as a way to experience the world beyond reservation borders and express their heritage as a warrior people. I met a sixteen-year-old who was riding in his fifth Crazy Horse Ride. His father noted that both he and his wife were veterans of US military service. He told me this year his son was riding to honor his older sister who was presently active in the US military.

The Crazy Horse Ride also carries a deeper symbolism beyond the honoring of modern-day veterans. When Crazy Horse rode into Fort Robinson to negotiate the best conditions of surrender for his people, he was killed and never got to ride out. Every rider and horse in the Crazy Horse Ride for the past eighteen years has ridden out of Fort Robinson as a living, breathing symbol of the ride Crazy Horse never got to take. The riderless horse that usually leads the ride can also be seen as a symbol of Crazy Horse. This deeper symbolism made their ride out of Fort Robinson one of the most compelling experiences of my life. In some sense it felt like they were riding to honor the ideal of freedom itself. It did not feel dramatic so much as resolute, something that was essential for them — and all of us.

The Oglala Lakota of Pine Ridge remain a strong and honorable people. All Americans are blessed that American Indians have persisted despite Euro-American policies of extermination, assimilation, and isolation on remote reservations.

Love and wisdom: [4]

My heart knows Crazy Horse did his best, but his story feels incomplete. Uneasiness remains in my heart because his people's freedom was taken away. This weekend at Fort Robinson was a poignant reminder of the moral debt Euro-American society owes to the American Indians and African slaves who paved the way for our ascendance. There are sad histories to be apologized for, wounds to be forgiven, and opportunities for great blessings to unfold, on the day all Americans live their lives and dreams in full freedom.

Wild Heart of Light

In the midst of writing about Crazy Horse, an urgent feeling interrupted me, "I've got to feel the Earth." My soul was calling me to sit with the sunset over Colorado's foothills and mountains. The late spring evening was cool with a brisk south breeze, so I grabbed two small meditation blankets for comfort as I settled into the scene. They were familiar friends with good memories and energy; one was a red and black light wool plaid purchased from a Maasai villager in Kenya a few years earlier. The other was a soft blue fleece printed with penguins.

Our west-facing deck was a thirty-eight by twelve-foot aerie looking across West Plum Creek valley to the foothills and

---

4   Many of the book's essays have a section called *Love and wisdom* to highlight the teachings received from the experiences described

beyond to Colorado's Front Range. The view was a hundred-twenty miles wide including three fourteeners: Pikes Peak, near Colorado Springs, Mt. Evans, near Denver, and Long's Peak in Rocky Mountain National Park. Mt. Evans was the centerpiece of that scene; a symbol of my love of mountains and Mother Earth. The striking cloud shapes to its north were glorious shades of magenta, peach, and red. There was a small dark cloud in front of the colors that seemed for a moment to be a symbol of my death. It was disturbing, but then it thinned and dissipated. Its message affirmed that death is not darkness and that it has no power over the light that is my essence.

Since a wilderness rafting trip twenty-five years ago, I had held the romantic notion that it would be the perfect symbol for my life's meaning, if at death, my ashes were scattered over the headwaters of the Tatshenshini River in Canada's Yukon. I would in some sense become part of that magnificent wild Eden. It was a good plan, but this evening a more feasible and equally satisfying plan was given.

In a vision, my wife, our daughters, and grandchildren were gathered at the top of Mount Evans at sunset to disperse my ashes. There was a brisk south wind, just like this summer evening, as they shook the container empty facing the sunset. My ashes simply blew away into that wild heart of light, the very symbol of who I am. A golden eagle was circling against the sky, crying its call of unbounded freedom to signal my beloveds that all was well with my soul.

After the vision I sat for a moment in quiet reverie. Then the closing revelation became clear in my heart; Crazy Horse's truth is just as described by Black Elk at the beginning of this chapter. He still rides in the wild realm of light; he and his horse are unfettered and free as the wind. All that was needed to heal his pain lives eternally within that realm. His soul is well and at peace. "Alleluia!" was all I could say. "Alleluia!"

History Lesson

I have often thought about the indigenous people who called North America home before the arrival of the Europeans. How might life have turned out for them, if, by some miracle, Turtle Island (North America) had remained isolated until the twenty-first century?

History is clear that the European invaders treated those who were already here with contempt rooted in fear, ignorance, and greed. Our ancestors carried out horrific acts, even including genocide. Acts of retribution were plentiful on both sides. In some ways, the Indians might have been better off if the Earth was *flat* and Columbus had sailed off the edge. But Columbus was right; the Earth is round and he succeeded in opening the Americas to colonization and exploitation. The results of that world-changing discovery are beautifully summarized in two remarkable books by Charles C. Mann, titled *1491* and *1493*.

One of the most devastating impacts of early European explorers was the introduction of diseases previously unknown in the Americas. They traveled farther and faster than the invaders' direct intrusions. For example, in 1682 when the French explorer LaSalle reached the town of Cahokia, east of present-day St. Louis in southern Illinois, he found an empty ghost town. Its fifteen thousand residents had been exterminated by smallpox long before his arrival.[ix]

Estimates of pre-Columbian native population in North America range up to twenty million living in balance with its resources across the entire continent. They were far more than simple hunter-gatherers living in an isolated Eden. The wilderness of the Americas was intentionally managed by its residents to optimize their food supplies, and other factors important to them.[x] Their numbers were already dramatically collapsed by the time the first New England colonists arrived one hundred twenty-eight years after Columbus. The wild forests they encountered were a result of the American Indian population collapse. Today it is estimated that two to four million American Indians remain, but inner-racial marriages and dispersal have made their numbers difficult to define and track. This decimation of numbers strongly suggests that they would have been better off had they remained undiscovered another five hundred years.

We know little about intertribal relations amongst America's tribes prior to Columbus' arrival. The violence that led the Europeans to characterize the American Indians as "savages" stems from *their* history of interactions with the native populations, not inter-tribal interactions. We tend to forget that the Indians were being invaded! By the time our pioneer ancestors directly encountered the Plains Indians, they had already been pushed west by neighboring tribes to their east, who themselves had moved west in response to the invasion of Europeans. That cascading process had created many intrusions and pressures amongst the Indian tribes before our ancestors ever encountered them. In the time of our Civil War, many Lakota, Dakota, and Nakota still lived in their traditional Minnesota homeland. They resisted the white intrusion and a number of them were taken prisoner. Dozens of them were executed as an example, ironically with the direct approval of President Abraham Lincoln. After that, the remaining Sioux fled to join their relatives who had already migrated into what is now the Dakotas, Nebraska, and Wyoming. Their migration created problems with all the tribes they displaced. Feelings between the Sioux and Crow tribes remain strained to this day.

As our ancestors arrived on North America's East Coast and began to move west, we directly or indirectly created the *Indian problem* we encountered. As we won our War for Independence, they were already losing theirs. From their perspective, the Europeans were invaders. That is how the United States acquired its *Indian problem*. When we consider our nation's history, it is good to remember it was written by the winners. As long as there have been winners and losers, the loser's story has often been very different and frequently remains untold.

Not all aspects of the European invasion were negative for the native people. Small horses had existed in North America for millennia, having crossed the land bridge from Siberia during the ice ages, along with the ancestors of the indigenous people later encountered by Europeans. Those early adventurers into the

Americas never knew the horse as a companion or workmate. They had only been considered game to be killed and eaten. They were smaller and apparently easier to hunt than many of the mega fauna of earlier times — enormous beasts like mammoths, mastodons, and giant bison that stood eight feet at the shoulder. In fact, the North American horse had been extinct for several millennia when the Spanish conquistadors reintroduced significantly larger horses to the Americas as warhorses. Were it not for that unintentional reintroduction, the marvelous horse culture of the Plains Indians could never have developed. The tremendous mobility and freedom of their glory years would have been something very different. Crazy Horse, as we have come to know him, would have had a different name, and undoubtedly, a very different story. Crazy Horse without a horse is as unthinkable as Columbus without a ship. In a very real sense, Crazy Horse had a horse *because* Columbus had a ship.

One could speculate that the decimation of American Indian life might never have happened if Europeans had not come until five hundred years later. But that idea is only hypothetical and has limited relevance for today's world. When all is said and done, humans don't have the capacity to change the past. It is obvious that the arrival of the Europeans was unmanaged and chaotic, with violence and vengeance by both colonists and American Indians often characterizing their interactions. It is sad, but probably unavoidable, that our ancestors' eagerness for a better life, along with fear of those they didn't know, left little room for wisdom or compassion. It was a violent and dangerous time; colonization usually is. But it seems unlikely that any of us, living in the context of those days, would have had the wisdom to write a better script.

Love and Wisdom:

The best choice left to us is to accept our history and focus our energy on how all Americans can trust each other and interact with fairness, respect, and dignity in the twenty-first century. The future is wide open for us to shape, but that process will only function well if it includes all Americans respectfully listening to each other and working together. It would be wonderful if we could open our hearts to let the power of love catalyze a twenty-first century movement toward balance and respect amongst all races and species of life living on this beautiful planet! The time is ripe and the idea is possible. The choice is ours to make.

Crow Country

The "Welcome to Crow Country" sign flashed by as I left Wyoming and entered Montana. According to Wikipedia, the Crow reservation covers about 3600 square miles. It is home to 7900 Crow tribal members out of approximately 11,000 who live in Montana.[xi] Even though I was driving in a light mist at interstate speeds, I sensed a subtle shift in the land's sense of itself as I entered the reservation. It seemed to feel more relaxed and appreciated; free from human manipulation and expectations. What I could see of it from I-90 was grassy brownish-green hills, with pine trees on north-facing slopes, gulleys filled with deciduous brush, and scattered brush on the hill tops. This is big country that cries out for one to mount a horse and ride and ride. You could ride those 3600 square miles for years and not lay eyes on all the wrinkles in Crow Country's corner of Mother Earth. This was originally the land of bison, now tamed to cattle country. There were only a few scattered Angus in my view that day, but the Crow have recently, after a century and a half absence, reintroduced bison on their reservation, a meaningful step in deep harmony with their heritage. It is a blessing for all of us who care about Mother Earth's natural flow of life.

The reservation land does feel like less is expected of it than the ranchlands outside Crow Country. Indigenous people remember that productivity and profit were not part of the original conversation between humans and the land. There is a feeling of sadness in the air over what has been lost combined with a faint sense of hope for what may yet be. I feel an audacious freedom quenched but not forgotten, and a sense of beauty hidden behind stoic faces. Trust has been lost and friendship remains largely undiscovered. The chance to show respect and build trust has been long buried beneath our collective fear. By now, for most of us, the opportunity is altogether absent from our awareness. For the most part, White and American Indian alike still carry enough fear to keep us separate and distant. Reconciliation remains suspended above a divide so wide and intractable that those on either side accept it as the way things are, with little consideration for building a bridge.

Love and wisdom:

The land outside of Crow Country is longing for the respect it finds within the boundary. The natural world and the love behind creation are quietly telling us that Indian and Euro-American reconciliation is a blessing waiting to happen for Mother Earth and all humanity. From an even bigger perspective, we are called to believe it is possible for all Americans to rebuild the trust that has been decaying over the centuries since Columbus, including the horrors of slavery that formally ended with our Civil War. Sadly, entrenched racial divisions have infected our society ever since our Euro-American ancestors first landed on these shores. To move forward, two things are required of us: We must be willing to make the effort and believe it is possible. It is a work of the heart. Are we ready?

A Shaman Friend

It felt like a reunion of old souls when Ruben Orellana and I met over a decade ago in Cusco, the ancient Inca capital in the Peruvian Andes. He had been retained as host and guide for our group visit to Machu Pichu and the Amazon. What an auspicious choice! Despite his biblical first name and Spanish surname, Ruben is a true Inca shaman, trained and deeply rooted in the mystical culture of his ancestors. He is also a university-trained archeologist, famous in Peru for the many startling discoveries made during his fourteen years as Head Archeologist at Machu Pichu. For Ruben, the union of shaman and archeologist facilitated a remarkable career. He relates with the ancient Inca world in ways not accessible to those who seek history but lack his shamanic training. His many discoveries at Machu Pichu, and how he found them, flowed through his flexible shamanic relationship with time and the non-physical realms of nature. He routinely did things that have no other explanation. For example, he used time travel during shamanic trance to visit Machu Pichu in its golden years when it was the spiritual retreat center for Inca royalty. Soon after, he would discover the archeological evidence for what he had seen. Ruben is also a gifted healer whose Well Spring Healing Center in Urubamba was known for marvelous results until he retired from that business. For these and many other reasons, Ruben is legendary in the Inca world and Peruvian Amazon. Meeting him opened the space within me to feel the power of nature way beyond what would otherwise have been possible. I am grateful.

This glimpse of my friend Ruben is shared as my personal witness to the power of a true shaman. He is a being of love, deeply anchored in the energies of the natural world. As our world careens toward an uncertain future, we expunge the world's indigenous cultures at our own peril. My love of nature and respect for their ancient ways of relating with nature tell me it is very important for all of us to treasure and trust the indigenous traditions that remain in this world. We don't have to adopt others' beliefs as our own, but it could be one of the world's shamans who throw all humanity a life-line in the face of a new pandemic, or who hauls us back from the precipice of environmental collapse. They simply understand the context of nature in ways that lie beyond the rest of us.

Besides resonating with American Indian connections to the natural world, I also feel deep sadness over the horrific way our ancestors treated the people that already occupied the Americas. Invasions, genocide, intentional lies, broken treaties, exploitation, and slavery do not make for an inspiring legacy. My understanding may be shallow and biased, but I know our ancestors could have done far better. Years ago, when I finished reading Dee Brown's *Bury my Heart at Wounded Knee*, I was so upset I was ready to go on the warpath — until I looked in the mirror. No wonder a gap in trust still festers between American Indians and the rest of us! Our shared history is as horrific as African slavery or the Jewish holocaust.

To get a glimpse of the vast changes brought to life on Planet Earth by the European discovery and subsequent colonization of the Americas, I recommend both of Charles C. Mann's books.[5] The story is still unfolding half a millennium later.

Love and wisdom:

I often ponder what we can do now to heal our nation's racial divides. Feeling sorry is barely a beginning. One hopes for a depth of reconciliation that is deeper than legalized gambling casinos and cheap cigarettes on reservations, and goes beyond legislative actions. It's hard to imagine further meaningful changes arising without sufficient trust to listen to each other. Is it too late to build some

5   *1491: New Revelations of the Americas Before Columbus* and *1493: Uncovering the New World Columbus Created*

soul-cleansing connections? How would we approach that? Are "we the people" sufficiently motivated to try? How would we start? What do you think?

Ganondagan

"The decisions we make today should result in a sustainable world seven generations into the future."
— Ancient Iroquois Wisdom

As a kid growing up in Western New York, my family lived in the heart of what had been Seneca Indian land for millennia. The native people of the area rarely came to mind, except when I asked about the names of many towns and rivers in our area that were Seneca in origin. I remember seeing a statue of Mary Jemison, "White woman of the Genesee," at Letchworth State Park a few times. She had been kidnapped by the Shawnee during a mourning ritual as a child, and adopted by the Seneca. She chose to remain a part of the tribe during the rest of her life, instead of returning to an American Colonial settlement.[xii] Today I believe that if Mary had been born a Seneca, there would be no statue and no memory of her beyond her Seneca descendants.

My mother was a naturally loving person who would have felt empathy for the native people, but my parents just didn't understand the Seneca role in our region's history or recognize their continuing presence in Western New York. The first white people who settled my home town in the late eighteenth century may well have encountered a few Seneca moving through their former land, but to my birth family any such memories were long forgotten. The Seneca were not in our awareness or part of our lives. This was similarly true for everyone we knew. American Indians were lost beyond the edges of Euro-American awareness in the Western New York of my youth.

Fifty miles away was the site of Ganondagan (pronounced Ga-NON-da-gan), the largest Seneca village in the seventeenth century. But I had never heard of Ganondagan until seventy-five years after my birth, when my sister Darlene suggested we visit the Seneca Art and Culture Center. I am deeply grateful to have finally found it, and an emerging sense of connection with our Seneca neighbors.

Ganondagan was described by seventeenth century missionaries as having 150 longhouses about a hundred feet long. Each longhouse belonged to a particular clan and could accommodate up to sixty people, so the population of Ganondagan may have been up to 9000. The Seneca had known as home much of what is now Western New York, long before the intrusion of Euro-American settlers. The name Ganondagan literally translates as "White Town." The name has no connection with the later flood of Euro-Americans that changed forever the life of all indigenous people in the Americas. In Seneca culture, white is associated with peace, so the translation they prefer today is "Town of Peace." Although Ganondagan was destroyed in the late seventeenth century by the French in a dispute over the lucrative fur trade, the name persists today as a New York State Historical Site, eighteen miles east of Rochester, near Victor, New York.[xiii]

On the last Sunday in October 2019, my sister and I visited the Seneca Art and Cultural center at Ganondagan to participate in an all-day cultural experience called *Restoring Our Food and Culture Through the Natural World.* [xiv] The auditorium held ten round tables, each with eight chairs, placed to facilitate a clear view of the speakers. Each table had one reserved chair for a guest whose lifework exemplified sustainable food relationships. Those guests would rotate amongst the tables between courses of the afternoon lunch, so the participants could meet several of them. Each table setting featured a placemat with beautiful illustrations of the *three sisters* (beans, corn, and squash) by a Seneca artist, Ellen Jemison. There was also a small handsewn cloth bag printed with pictures of ears of corn. Its open end was tied with a yellow ribbon with an attached tag. The tag was decorated with a drawing of the three sisters. It said, "The decisions we make today should result in a sustainable world seven generations into the future." Inside were reusable bamboo eating utensils and drinking straw, in perfect harmony with the tag's message. The organizers had orchestrated a perfect plan to help participants understand and accept the relationships with nature and food held by the Seneca, Potawatomi, and many indigenous cultures around the world.

The three presenters were each keepers and sharers of Mother Earth's wisdom by the way they live their lives. Their words and food carried welcome and wisdom from Mother Earth herself. There was a synergy amongst them that carried meaning beyond what each of them shared. Our Earth Mother was lifted up in the minds and hearts of all who participated. Peter Jemison (Heron Clan, Seneca), Historic Site Manager at Ganondagan State Historic Site, welcomed us and introduced the speakers. His presence did a masterful job of holding the sacred space within which the day unfolded. At the dedication of The Seneca Art & Culture Center in 2015 he noted:

> Our goal is to tell the world that we are not a people in the past tense. We live today. We have adapted to the modern world, but we still maintain our language, ceremonies, land base, government, lineages and culture. When you're a native person, your story is often told by other people. Here, we tell our own story. [xv]

Our day was organized around the speakers sharing part of their Seneca and Potawatomi culture. Their way of life is anchored in respect and gratitude for the natural world. My heart was singing all day as they shared aspects of their worldview; there was deep harmony with my own love for Mother Earth.

The gathering opened with Peter Jemison leading us in, "Words before All Else — Greetings to the Natural World," a traditional prayer that is spoken by an elder to open a gathering of the Seneca people. He explained each step of the prayer in English before speaking it in the Seneca language. In English, the opening stanza was printed on our placemats:

We are all thankful to our Mother, the Earth, for she gives us all that we need for life. She supports our feet as we walk about upon her. It gives us joy that she continues to care for us as she has from the beginning of time. To our mother we send our greetings and our thanks.[xvi]

The prayer then continued with individual gratitude for many beings (sun, moon, plants, and animals) that give their gifts to support the lives of the Seneca people. Because I grew up in Seneca country, I knew many of the beings the prayer honored. My heart felt the prayer's power and beauty despite not knowing the Seneca language. It brought me to the edge of tears as Peter spoke it.

The rest of the morning featured the keynote lecture from Robin Wall Kimmerer. Dr. Kimmerer is Distinguished Teaching Professor of Environmental and Forest Biology at the SUNY College of Environmental Science and Forestry and an enrolled member of the Citizen Band Potawatomi. She is also the founding Director of the Center for Native People and the Environment. Their mission is to create programs that combine both indigenous wisdom and scientific knowledge to address our shared concerns for Mother Earth. These expressions of her lifework are in perfect harmony with her cultural heritage. Dr. Kimmerer has become quite well-known through her two books, *Gathering Moss*, a winner of the John Burroughs Medal Award for Natural History Writing, and *Braiding Sweetgrass: Indigenous Wisdom, Scientific Knowledge, and the Teachings of Plants*. Both are so excellent they have garnered a wide audience. The internet is filled with accolades, but I prefer to speak of how her teaching skills and wisdom affected me.

Her presentation style involved mind and heart in equal measure. She was in constant eye contact with her audience and only referred to notes a few times in a talk that lasted well over an hour. As she spoke, her voice was gentle, and at the same time her use of language was precise. Rarely have I experienced a teacher who cared so much about her message *and* her audience. It felt like her mind was sharing treasures of indigenous wisdom, while at the same time her heart reached out and embraced us.

I offer my notes with the intention to faithfully reflect her feelings and meanings: In the Potawatomi language, all plants are collectively called *gifts* or *blessings*. In fact, the word for "berry" is the same as the word for "gift." Her remarks made it clear that the way we humans use language shapes the way we think about the food we eat. The Potawatomi think of themselves as the *younger brothers* of creation who receive the gifts of life and sustenance from plants and other creatures, who have been upon the Earth far longer than we have been here. Those of us tuned into western language and thought might consider domesticated plants and animals as "produce" or "meat" over whom we have been given dominion. We have understood dominion to mean our role was to dominate nature rather than cooperate with her as caretakers. In my thinking, we have even become comfortable manipulating plant and animal family heritage (DNA) to better serve what we perceive as our needs. We rarely think of the plant and animal kingdoms as the elders of creation and gifts that the Potawatomi know them to be.

To help this sink in, Dr. Kimmerer asked us to take two or three deep breaths. She then pointed out this truth; the oxygen our body inhales to survive is a gift exhaled by plants. We are breathing in their exhaled breath. When we exhale our breath, the carbon dioxide it contains is inhaled by plants to sustain their life process of photosynthesis. This sacred exchange is how plants create the gifts of food and shelter they provide to sustain us. That is how *inter*dependent we humans are with the natural world — we are part of it and cannot survive without it!

Her remarks on plants concluded with this: Unlike people, plants tell their story not by what they say, but by what they do. Plants teach in the universal language of food. What they teach us is who they are as a *people.* I think that for those who eat meat, the relationships seem more complex, but similar.

At one point in her lecture Robin asked us why we thought the Potawatomi braid sweetgrass? The participants fumbled around trying to guess the answer, so she finally bailed us out and told us they see sweetgrass as Mother Earth's hair. She then asked what it meant when they braid it?

Nearly three years ago, I was with two young women; sisters who are like honorary granddaughters to me. One was lying in a hospital bed in her final coma, dying of a malignant brain tumor at age twenty-six. The younger one kept trying to arrange her dying sister's hair to keep it from falling across her face. She finally ended up braiding her sister's hair. I have never seen a more tender expression of love. So, when Dr. Kimmerer asked what braiding sweetgrass meant, I blurted out, "It is an act of love."

That response seemed to resonate with what she was seeking.

Dr. Kimmerer closed her remarks by telling us how a Potawatomi elder responded when asked to describe an educated person. He responded that "An educated person is one who knows their gifts and how to give them away." She then told us if we want to understand our responsibilities to the world, we need only ask "What are our gifts?" Our responsibility is to know our gifts and give them to the world.[xvii]

If I had to express my take-away from Robin's lecture in one sentence it would be: We are not separate from nature in any way, so we are to love her like family.

After a break we resumed the meeting with a five-course lunch of authentic indigenous foods prepared under the direction of acclaimed chef, Loretta Barrett Oden, also a member of the Citizen Band Potawatomi. Lunch took most of the afternoon until the gathering closed. Ms. Oden's professional life has centered around her passion to restore, preserve, and document indigenous foods traditions around the world, including sources, recipes, and preparation techniques. Her aim is to restore the Potawatomi and other precontact (before Columbus) food traditions and relationships. She knows in her heart that this pathway is inherently healthier than typical twenty-first century food consumption norms. Ms. Barrett Oden has said, "All of my foods are pretty much precontact foods with a few sprinkles of modern-day ingredients."[xviii]

Her skills were evident in the wide array of dishes we enjoyed at lunch. All were based on the three sisters; corn, beans, and squash. The skilled preparation techniques with herbs and spices resulted in each dish having unique textures and flavors. We were served a five-course cafeteria-style lunch made almost entirely from the three sisters in multiple varieties. The first course was a green salad without the greens we would normally expect. It was mostly shredded zucchini, but much more appetizing than it first sounds. There was a modest addition of red kidney beans and red speckles of some herb with a noticeable but unfamiliar flavor; sort of bitter, but not strong enough to be disturbing. Despite initial trepidation, I actually enjoyed the salad. For me, its best feature was the vinaigrette dressing with its semi-sweet, bright sparkly flavor.

Next was butternut squash soup, hot and creamy smooth, with rich aroma highlights from skillfully chosen spices; I think I tasted cardamom and nutmeg. When Euro-Americans eat out we often are served bread or crackers with salad and soup. Here there were neither. Instead, the entire meal except dessert, was graced by a generous supply of perfectly baked, maple syrup-flavored corn bread. Both maple syrup and corn have been Iroquois staple foods for millennia. Its texture was firm, yet tender; you could actually pick it up and take a bite without a shower of crumbs in your lap. Yum!

The next two courses were stew and stir fry both made with similar varieties of the three sisters. Summer squashes (zucchini and yellow crookneck) were the most prevalent ingredient. Corn and beans were also present in a supporting role, bringing their varieties of nutrition, texture, and flavor. The texture of the stew was chunkier, while the stir fry was more shredded. Either could have been a main course, but most people took modest servings of both. Their flavors were distinctively different. The stew tasted more traditional and substantial, more like I would think of as a main course, while the stir fry was lighter and spicier. The red flecks in it likely were hot peppers, but the heat was not excessive.

The meal was topped off with a dessert of cornbread pudding topped with fresh raspberries, a personal favorite. Drinks options included tea, coffee, and water flavored with lemon and mint. It was quite surprising to find such a variety of flavors and textures in a vegetarian meal prepared from only three families of ingredients. Eating a precontact meal created with Barrett Oden's skill was delightful; my taste buds were happy all afternoon. After this meal we understood how she and her eldest son ran a successful restaurant for twenty-five years in Santa Fe, NM featuring traditional indigenous cuisine from around the world.

Both Dr. Kimmerer and Ms. Barrett Oden emphasized their belief that native people would benefit greatly from taking responsibility for their own food supply and quality. The same is true for all of us. The speakers also emphasized that eating organic food, preferably from our own garden, is a far healthier and cost-effective option than a typical supermarket. Today's workshop demonstrated how delicious it can be.

My sister and I agreed that our participation in this event was one of our better choices in a long time. We are grateful to the Seneca and Potawatomi nations, all the presenters, and participants; and especially Mother Earth.

Love and wisdom:

This delightful day at Ganondagan cemented more solidly my conviction that the indigenous people of the world hold, and have held for millennia, a relationship with Mother Earth that could profoundly bless the rest of us and Mother Earth. The workshop reinforced my connection with American Indian ideals and beliefs. Yet, understanding how this experience will inform my life pathway remains elusive. Because I trust life as a process that unfolds in harmony with my path, this lack of clarity seems okay, at least for now. I know my direction is toward love, and have come to love Mother Earth like close family. I also have an ache in my heart for racial and gender reconciliation. Creation Is a Love Song is a piece of my pathway, as was this cultural experience at Ganondagan. The reason for these activities is to facilitate a paradigm shift toward love. I am called to share who I am and trust the inner voice of my soul to inspire and guide me. So long as I remain open and enthusiastic about my pathway and intention, opportunities will continue to arise. I need only say "yes" as they are revealed. But I am responsible for knowing when to speak my "yes." That is true for each of us.

CHAPTER 2
FINDING SACRED WISDOM IN NATURE

Much of our relationship with nature is an ongoing flow of impressions so frequent and common our awareness doesn't notice. This is good — it keeps us from being overwhelmed by too much information for our brains to process. But these limits of our awareness automatically bypass much of our experience of life. And even events exceptional enough to remember are only the surface of the story. Everything in creation, including our life, is multifaceted far beyond where our five senses can reach. So, one must often look beyond the obvious to find the deeper aspects of life. The following stories share a few of my meaningful experiences.

Baptism

"Coincidences are spiritual puns."
G.K. Chesterton, *Irish Impressions*

On a beautiful day a few Octobers ago, the loud screech of a yellow-shafted flicker lured us outside. We briefly admired his vibrant colors as he flew away, his assignment accomplished. Just then, a scream from the heavens announced a pair of red-tail hawks soaring above. Their tail feathers seemed brighter than real in the intense sunlight. We were mesmerized as they slowly circled higher. I recalled two stories related by friends when red-tail hawks had apparently acted as spirit guides to encourage departing souls to let go and engage their journey home. I joked about hoping this pair hadn't come for us! With marvelous insight, my wife Marilyn remarked that maybe they came to reassure us that everything was okay with our friends. Bill had passed away three days before and I would officiate his memorial service three days hence. Gwen, his wife of 60 years, survived.

Then the baptism happened. From the same spot in the sky, first one hawk and then the other ejected an anal squirt brightly backlit by the sun. The droplets fell directly toward us as they fragmented into finer and finer pieces and momentarily disappeared. Suddenly the air was full of tiny wisps and micro droplets of light floating down all around us. They were too small to feel, but some of them surely landed on both of us. An inexplicable feeling of awe arose; something sacred had just happened and it was over before we even realized it. It was an amazing moment but we had little hope of understanding what it meant. Yet, we were in a state of bedazzled gratitude; we had just been baptized by the pair of red-tails — a magical moment that transcended time and understanding.

Love and wisdom:

Later a sense of clarity was given about what the baptism might mean. It would be perfectly consistent with Bill's wild and weird sense of humor to express his gratitude for our friendship and support of his family with a hawk poop baptism. It was beautiful and meaningful; at the same time, it was a poop shower. We will never know whether this interpretation is accurate, but it would have been no surprise to hear Bill chuckling in the background.

Wilderness as Teacher: A Personal Memoir[6]

I cannot say when it began, but the sense of something important *out there* has been with me from an early age. There is an unfocused memory of a small boy standing at the upstairs window wondering at the wooded hills overlapping behind my parent's house. The feelings I recall were wanting to be there, deeply called to explore those hills; all this also accompanied by frustration. Dad was too busy to take me and Mom thought I was too young to go.

A decade later my world was larger, the hills smaller and more accessible to a teenager trying to prove he could do the same things as men. Hiking, camping, cooking over a wood fire, catching trout, trapping, and hunting all became ways to demonstrate that I was

---

6   I recently rediscovered this essay written half a lifetime ago. Two things surprised me; I was a decent writer that long ago and its relevance persisted so long. The essay reminded me that the natural world has long been a key setting for my spiritual growth.

growing up. Horizons were defined by dreams shared with friends. Growing up in Western New York, wilderness lived to the north; the Adirondacks in my home state, and beyond to the endless wilds of Canada and Alaska. That was the wild terrain that held our dreams. We talked of hunting cabins in Canada and driving used cars to Alaska for quick money and adventure. We made plans about being in faraway places filled with moose, bears, and wolves.

In my mid-teens, a neighborhood friend and I had occasional *outdoor sleep-overs* in our backyard. We sometimes looked up at the heavens through binoculars just to feel the edge of infinity. The night sky was a vast panorama; awe-inspiring beyond our capacity to even imagine what we were seeing. This was several years before astronauts and space travel, so the words were not even available in our heads to talk about it. It made our earthly home seem so tiny and isolated. So instead, we talked about earth-bound dreams of things we would do when we were grown-ups.

The Milky Way was an obvious broad band of light across the heavens from one horizon to the other, shining forth from the matrix of stars that seemed to hold it in place. With binoculars, the concentration of stars was almost staggering; maybe ten times what the unaided eye could see. I wondered how it was possible for astronomers keep track of so many. One summer night, we were excited to see a bright star drift across the still pattern of stars from west to east — a satellite! It took only three minutes or so from the time we spotted it until it was beyond our corner of the sky. This remarkable occasion had to have happened in 1958. There were no man-made satellites before that summer; Russia's Sputnik 1, the first satellite in Earth orbit, was launched on October 4, 1957, with Sputnik 2 later that year. With cold war urgency, the U.S. launched Explorer 1 on February 1, 1958 and the space race was on. I graduated from high school in 1959, and with a brand-new driver's license, I was a busy young man chasing girls and anticipating college. Backyard sleepovers were suddenly passé, so 1958 was the only summer it could have been. It seems amazing that today, barely six decades later, the sky is so filled with satellites that NASA has to worry about collisions.

It often seems such dreams grow best when we are young. Too soon life pushes our dreams aside to make way for the practical considerations of adulthood. Education, careers, and family responsibilities gather us into cities and their suburbs. If we're lucky, we can see mountains or forests from an office window or on the drive home — when we remember to look. The need to honor our responsibilities consumes our sense of mystery, and wilderness feels remote. Wild places we once knew, or dreamed of, are pushed off in time or forgotten. Today, more and more of us are born in cities and spend our lives barely knowing what we are missing.

In spite of growing isolation from wilderness, its distant whispers can send tremors of longing through our inner reaches. My first visit to Yellowstone awakened feelings long dormant. I became a prodigal son, returning home to a place long imagined, but never seen. Mother Earth's steamy thermal eruptions were impressive, but a bit scary. I wasn't used to Mother Earth acting so unstable and angry. Besides that, omnipresent signs warned visitors to stay on the boardwalks, because the crust was so thin, a person might break through it. If that was true, what might burst through from below!? Except for Old Faithful, the eruptions were quite random, so turning your back felt risky. Clouds of steam seemed to be everywhere, often accompanied by sulphureous fumes that reminded me of rotten eggs.

I much preferred the pastoral views of abundant elk and bison, with an occasional soaring bald eagle or foraging grizzly bear. But my favorite animals in Yellowstone were trumpeter swans, the largest species of swan on Earth. Despite their size and weight, they carried themselves with unspeakable power and grace. Their snow-white feathers stood out against the blue lake like an etching, while the arc of their neck and fluid motion when gliding across its surface was a symphony unfolding. One can't help being impressed watching a trumpeter race across the water with wings flapping to launch from the water into the sky. The racket of its legs splashing and the beating of their nearly ten-foot wingspan sounded like a small helicopter. It takes a lot of effort to self-hurtle a 15 to 30-pound bird body into the sky. Indeed, the bald eagle was only the second most impressive bird we saw in Yellowstone.

The memories of that first visit are etched so deeply they border on pain. Some part of me is still in Yellowstone and something of Yellowstone remains in me. Its wildness still calls me to be there again, and again.

Remarkable as it is, Yellowstone is not singular in its ability to excite those who are moved by nature's grandeur. The first time I saw the Grand Canyon, it was with a group of friends who had driven to a campground near the North Rim and set up camp.

It was a cool evening with no wind, and the pines were quietly sharing their scent with the world. Dinner was eaten and it was moving toward dusk. My tent was ready to welcome me for sleep, when curiosity drew me to meander along a quiet, lightly used path through the tall Ponderosa pines. With a cover of pine needles, it held no sense of urgency to take one somewhere. Then suddenly, with no fence or warning, the forest disappeared into a great yawning abyss of fading red and graying depths and purple shadows. The familiar hollow spot in my solar plexus from being too near an abrupt edge made my knees feel weak. My body always responds to high edges that way and I have never found a way to prepare for their impact. I simply sat there awe-struck with my back against one of the pines, while the light slowly evaporated. I don't think I could have moved until darkness broke the spell.

There have been other times and places; a series of bright moments, sometimes tainted by fear of potential decline and loss. Wilderness presents a myriad of faces within fragile borders and shrinking boundaries. There is vast power in its weather and waters; fierce vulnerability in its wild creatures.

Betatakin, Keet Seel, Tsega, Chaco, de Chelly — canyon names in the Four Corners region feel strange on the tongue of an Anglo from the northeastern U.S. Here the land is old, long used; and by some, long abandoned and forgotten. Wilderness has been reborn, not by intent, but through neglect. Anasazi towns, with their fields, buildings, and irrigation systems, have gradually been reclaimed by juniper, pinon, mule deer, jackrabbits, and coyotes. Above all there lingers a sense of clues missed and trails faded. There are people who abandoned the Four Corners region and apparently vanished over seven hundred years ago. There is an emptiness of the soul here. The Anasazi canyons feel lonely.

The St. Joe River flows into Lake Coeur d'Alene in Idaho's panhandle. This has always been great fishing country with several records that have stood the test of time. Each spring, nomadic fishermen return whose ancestors have fished here for millennia. The St. Joe River supports the largest nesting colony of ospreys in North America. The great fish eagles wheel over the waters, diving with controlled chaos to catch trout and salmon. Their young are hatched among sticks piled high in the branches of almost every tall tree along the river. There are hundreds of ospreys, each one a striking symbol of clean unspoiled wilderness. It is hard to remember we nearly lost all of them to pesticide poisoning only a few years ago. The St. Joe would still have been beautiful without the ospreys; with them it is remarkable.

In the decades following the 1859 discovery of gold in the Colorado Rockies, dozens of timberline basins in Colorado's San Juan Range were ravaged by extensive mining activity. The trees for miles around were cut for rail ties, mine timbers, and cabins. High mountain meadows became mudholes and spoil piles.

Yankee Boy Basin is a high mountain valley ringed by the Sneffle's Range on the north and a lesser ridge to the south. The miners tore it up worse than most. When the gold was gone, they walked away, leaving a hellish ecological mess. Yet today, a century later, Yankee Boy buzzes, hums, and clicks for two months every summer. The basin plays host to a pilgrimage of bees, hummingbirds, and photographers each July and August. Columbine, alpine daises, asters, rosy paintbrush, elephant head, larkspur, and other flower species cover whole mountainsides. There are square miles of flowers growing so thickly, it was impossible for me to avoid crushing some with every step. I felt guilty, but there were so many and their beauty so profound, that I was mesmerized and compelled. I just *had* to keep walking to see more. The bees and birds seemed to feel similar unbridled enthusiasm.

The legend is told of a particular gentleman who broadcast hundreds of pounds of wildflower seeds each summer for several years in the early 1900s. Whether or not that story is true, nature's recreative powers have brought the slow quiet triumph of the flowers. In early August, there is no place on Earth more beautiful.

High above the abandoned mine rubble at Silver Pick Basin, along a steep section of the Wilson Peak trail, there was a columbine plant with three flowers growing next to the base of a small cliff. Its life energy was vibrantly on display with deep green leaves and bright blooms with blue petals and yellow stamens. Even though columbine flowers don't have a pronounced scent, there was a presence about this plant, a feel of pride saying, "Here I am, notice me." And I did.

Trickling snow-melt kept the granite damp enough to support a backdrop of dark green moss. A white and brown speckled feather, lost from the breast of a ptarmigan, was sent tumbling down the cliff face by a puff of breeze. It touched the right-hand flower, hesitated for perhaps a second, and fell to a lower leaf stem on the same plant. In perfect stillness it stayed there, impossibly suspended from an invisible point. After it was photographed, I sat watching the feather for nearly an hour. It was still hanging when I left. The odds that I was in that place, at that time, and actually noticed the feather, felt like a miracle. Sometimes wilderness speaks its beauty most distinctly in a whisper.

Because such wilderness experiences have held strong meaning for me, it seems important that I understand the lessons that they carry. How can one hope to describe what ospreys, wildflowers, trumpeter swans, and a ptarmigan feather have in common with Yellowstone or the great canyon cut through Arizona's Kaibab Plateau? Yet, all of them can be seen as facets of the same essence: an expression of the natural world in a pure, unspoiled form.

Love and wisdom:

I cannot say why wild places bless the center of my being; neither can I ignore the fact that they do. Perhaps we must relearn an ancient truth our ancestors knew by heart; that we humans are also part of the natural world. We came into being within its context and cannot exist apart from it. When I am in wilderness, it brings an inner comfort; the peace of returning home from a long journey. May it always be so.

Canyon Communion

"Nature is the art of God".
–Sir Thomas Browne, *Religioso Medici*

Waterton Canyon is a marvelous recreation corridor cut by the South Platte River through the Rocky Mountain foothills south of Denver. On a sunny day in late winter, I went for a walk there with the intention to move slowly and notice whatever nature had to share. After three miles, I sat on a river-bank tree root in quiet harmony with my surroundings. A sense of oneness with the natural world seeped into me.

My new hearing aids brought higher pitched sounds not heard in years, as the river sang and bubbled its way downstream. It was like my ears had only been aware of the low and mid-range sounds of an orchestra for years, when suddenly the high notes were also present, like someone plucking the strings of a violin. When I closed my eyes, I realized that its sounds were particular to the contours of the streambed, the volume and speed of water flow, the slope downriver, and so on. On this day the South Platte's language seemed just beyond my comprehension, but at that moment, I imagined its voice saying, "I am the South Platte River sharing this place with you. No other spot along this river, or any other river in all the Cosmos, carries precisely the sounds you are hearing right here, right now." That river music would have been innately beautiful in any time and place, but realizing I was *actually sharing* it with the river in the moment, made it transcendent. That experience and that moment on the South Platte River had never happened before, nor will it ever again be perfectly replicated, at any place or time in the entire life of the Universe. Every one of our moments is equally unique. How sad that we miss so much by placing our attention elsewhere than this moment.

Shadows and erratic chirping tell me chickadees are flitting among the upper branches of the tree whose root I'm seated upon. It's a mystery how these small feathered descendants of the dinosaurs ever made it to the twenty-first century. After an enormous asteroid or comet slammed into Mother Earth sixty-six million years ago, huge tsunamis, extraordinary earthquakes, and dramatic changes in atmosphere and weather all around the planet, caused a great extinction of life, perhaps in as little as ten years.[xix] While ten years is barely a moment in geologic time, it is estimated that three-quarters of all plant and animal species on Earth went extinct during that cataclysm, including most of the larger more powerful ancestor species of my chickadee friends. Besides the direct impact of bone-chilling cold, weather changes wiped out much of the food supply, so many reptiles and other species disappeared forever into the abyss of extinction. It feels miraculous that chickadees and their kin are even here. What were the odds?

A small white stone rests just to my left. Sunlight dancing with its fine quartz crystals caught my eye. The individual crystals are actually clear, but their myriad interfaces and micro fractures reflect the light in ways that make the stone opaque and look similar to milk glass, only with sparkles. It is only a couple of inches long and not sufficiently smooth to be a typical river rock. I wonder how long it's been here in the canyon and whether it originated in the mountains a hundred miles upstream. Probably it was orphaned from its mother rock by glaciers during the ice ages that ended several millennia ago. Regardless of its history, the rock was so pretty I brought it home to show our friends that evening. One of them saw the shape of a face in its contours; something I had missed entirely. Life often offers more to see if we look a second time.

My foot had been resting on a football sized chunk of granite until it slid a foot further down the riverbank. It exposed fresh soil that had been sheltered until then. I wondered what tiny, even microscopic, bits of life had been exposed to evaporation and cold. Something is likely to die because I caused a rock to slide a foot downhill. We humans are always upsetting something's life just by being here. The same is true of everything else. While life taken as a whole is robust and vibrant, individual expressions of it can be delicate, even tenuous. There is deep wisdom in remembering that we are part of this web of life.

Of all things to notice here today are two flies. A fat one and a skinny one just landed on my journal page and back of my hand. What are they doing zipping around here in February? It was well below freezing last night and is only in the mid-40s now. It will freeze again tonight. Where do they find shelter? What do they eat? Flies truly seem to be ubiquitous. Just then, the skinny one came back to re-emphasize the mystery of its life — or maybe just to be admired. Creation is an amazing array!

Love and wisdom:

This day reminded me how important it is to be very quiet, inside and out, when exploring. I miss way too much when I move too fast. Sometimes walking slowly is way too fast. To be still allows my awareness to merge into oneness with nature. That common ground is always present when I take time to notice.

Conversations

A month later, I began another walk in Waterton Canyon with the same intent to be quiet and pay attention to nature. A popular attraction in the canyon is its herd of Rocky Mountain Bighorn Sheep. I had seen over thirty of them earlier that year. Today I encountered a smaller herd of about a dozen ewes and lambs, along with one adolescent ram that had appointed himself their security guard. They were hanging out in the middle of the gravel access road to Strontia Springs Dam, a Denver Water Board impoundment. I knew they were either heading to the river to drink or returning to the security of the steep canyon side after drinking, but I couldn't sense their intended direction. They stood facing me as the young ram moved to the front of the herd staring directly at me. There was a momentary standoff. So, I spoke to him, "Well, what's it going to be? Which way are you going? I'm not here to cause trouble. I just want to go on up the road." I spoke with confidence in my deep baritone voice, but not in a loud or threatening way. His response was to briefly mount one of the ewes. It was six months out of synch with breeding season, so I took it that he was telling me these were his family and it was his job to protect them from deep-voiced strangers. I slowly walked a few steps along the left edge of the road (not directly at him) to convey my desire to pass by his herd between them and the river. In unison he and the other sheep looked away from me to face the canyon wall. This seemed a clear signal of their permission for me to pass. I did so while thanking them in that same deep baritone voice. We had communicated clearly with no feeling of fear on either side. I looked back from a respectful distance as they walked down the riverbank for their drink. It was strange and wonderful to realize I just had a meaningful conversation with a herd of wild bighorn sheep. It had been so natural and effortless, I didn't realize what had happened until thinking about it afterward.

An hour later, my planned lunch spot along the river was already occupied by a pair of Canadian geese resting in the grass. So, I sat at a table in a picnic pavilion seventy feet away while we watched each other. After a bit they decided I wasn't a threat and the smaller one (female) began to graze the new grass along the riverbank. The male stayed between me and its mate keeping watch. After several minutes the female began to graze gradually in my direction. I softly told her how brave she was to keep moving closer. When only about five feet away she made a low croaking sound deep in her throat; I mimicked the sound. The goose repeated; so did I. It uttered several different sounds and I did my best to echo them back — all of this with direct eye contact between us. This went on for several minutes with the male resting and watching on the cement floor ten feet away. Finally, they wandered off to continue grazing. We had shared a conversation in goose language and I have no idea what was communicated other than this: We were completely comfortable sharing the same picnic shelter. Afterwards while I was sitting on the riverbank recording the experience in my journal, the pair flew by, landed on the river, swam across, and disappeared into the reeds. Maybe they will nest there later this spring.

Love and wisdom:

These two encounters were the experience with nature I was seeking. Both conversations were deeply profound, at least to me. When I was clear about my intention and open to how it would unfold, meaningful interactions with wild creatures came easier than I had expected. It was delightful to converse with my wild brothers and sisters. There was no way to know whether the conversations held meaning for the animals, however it made an imprint upon me.

Surf, Seals, and Sunsets

Today the ocean was "big." That was the term used by a local gentleman we met walking along the wild northern California coast. Strong northwest winds brought huge waves crashing ashore with power and roaring mayhem, so loud it was impossible to hear each other, the seals, or anything else. Its intensity brought us the smell and coolness of the great North Pacific; I could actually taste the salty mist.

In the midst of this tumultuous world, mother seals were doing their best to keep their newborn pups safe. To my wife and I, they looked very vulnerable in the gray churning waters, despite the graceful sleek movements of their streamlined deep-brown bodies. Because it would have been terrifying for us to be caught in those waters, it was hard to appreciate how well adapted seals are to life in the North Pacific. We saw a few mother-pup pairs in one sheltered cove, but most of the seals were in open water between the beach and off-shore rocks that partially buffered the raging waters. Normally they might find comfortable resting places on those off-shore rocks, but not today; every advancing wave-front buried them under tons of water.

At first it seemed odd that the seals avoided the shelter of the beaches during such a storm. As we walked along the cliff top looking down at them, they kept an eye on us all the time, very uneasy with our presence. Then I remembered; humans are the primary predator these seals have known for many generations, so they feel safer away from the beaches on off-shore rocks. Seals do use more secluded beaches, but avoid those frequented by people.

One might think most people have made peace with nature in the twenty-first century and question whether their caution was necessary. A few years ago, while walking a beach north of San Diego, I came upon a poignant scene. A dead sea lion had washed ashore with an obvious bullet hole in its side. Although its light-brown fur was dry, there was no odor of rotting flesh and the body was not yet bloated. It must have washed ashore within the past day or two. Someone had placed a circle of beach stones around the carcass and a driftwood cross near its head.

Some commercial fishermen kill sea lions and seals because they are seen as competition for their livelihood. Some abalone fishermen shoot sea otters for the same reason. No wonder the seals were cautious with people around!

Big waves make for great sunset pictures when the setting sun ignites clouds formations. But clouds were sparse the week we were there, so the only color came when mist hanging over the ocean turned the setting sun into a big ball. As it sank toward the horizon, it slowly turned from yellow to orange, and finally a deep crimson. Beautiful colors reflected from the smoother water between the wave fronts as they rolled toward the beach. The colors were more visible up on the cliffs; down on the beach the waves blocked our view of the reflections.

Love and wisdom:

The ocean spoke a parable about life itself; Whether or not we see life's beauty depends on how we look at it.

Lord, Give Me Patience

"Trees are sanctuaries ... they preach, unde-
terred by particulars, the ancient law of life."
— Hermann Hesse, *Wandering: Notes and Sketches*

Several years ago, we visited the trees in Humboldt Redwoods State Park just inland from the northern California coast. It houses a royal remnant of Mother Earth's tree kingdom, scattered in several modest preserves amid what was once a vast empire along North America's Pacific Coast. Redwood trees have graced the planet for 240 million years and, under optimum conditions, individual trees can live over two thousand years. Their potential size is staggering, with the tallest one in today's world standing at 380 feet. Just four such trees standing end-to-end would be taller than the Empire

State Building. Their maximum trunk circumference can reach 75 feet; I am over six feet tall with an arm span to match, and it would still take a dozen people my size touching fingertips to reach around such a tree. Another statistic to stretch your imagination: such a tree would weigh 800 tons — that's 40 semis with trailers loaded to maximum capacity!

While none of the trees in the Humboldt Preserve are that large, several approach it. Their thick weathered gray bark is usually free from branches for the first hundred feet or more. Sunlight is so limited on the forest floor that branches lower down would contribute only minimal photo-synthesis and nutrition. Over the centuries, growing trees gradually eliminate the lower branches as their usefulness fades.

In apparent humility, perhaps to compensate for their enormous size, redwood foliage is fine and feathery compared to most conifers. Bending back to look up at these trees, the shaded areas were a deep jade green with contrasting bright chartreuse where sunlight struck the upper canopy. The accompanying evergreen aroma added its touch to the peaceful ambiance of the giant trees. We walked among them in silent reverence, taking picture after picture, knowing all the time that no camera could capture the awe we were feeling. I believe all of Mother Earth is sacred, but being in this grove brought uncommon awareness of that truth.

At one point I sat on a bench to be with the trees in silence. My eyes were closed as my awareness merged with their presence. After a while I was moved to ask them the secret of their legendary longevity. "Be patient" was the silent response. My next thought was, "How can I better serve Mother Earth and all life?" Again, the same answer, "Be patient." I asked a few more related questions and the answer was always, "Be patient."

I suppose their guidance is rooted in their life experience. Many of the trees in this preserve have been standing straight and tall for well over a millennium. In another redwood preserve, a tree recently died that had twenty-five hundred annual growth rings. To put that age in perspective, that particular redwood emerged from its mother seed four centuries *before* Jesus was born. It might be living still had not some entrepreneur cut a portal for tourists to drive their cars through! During their long lives, old growth redwoods have withstood drought, floods, windstorms, and wildfires while they simply grew above and beyond lesser trees. Experience taught them there was enough time to grow so far toward the light that neighboring trees would eventually struggle in their shadows or die. Being patient has served these ancient ones well.

For many twenty-first century humans, patience is fleeting at best. Most of us have been trained from early childhood that life must be organized and controlled so there's enough time to get everything done. This approach provides endless urgency and busyness, often leaving people overworked, stressed out, and isolated from life's joy. When we don't dare to trust life, it feels like constant vigilance is required to keep it moving in the direction of our best interest. Does the redwoods' advice to "be patient" have any relevance in twenty-first century America?

If patience is to be a feasible option for moving through life, we must learn to trust life. I once read a Yogi Tea bag tag that said,

"Trust is the union of intelligence and integrity." That seems right; unless we believe a person possesses both characteristics, we will not trust them. But, do such characteristics fit an ancient tree? When I think about a millennia-old redwood, it feels like the answer is yes; I am comfortable trusting them. Whether or not to trust their advice is tied to whether I trust my own capacity to discern their message. Did I simply imagine it, or was it real? Applied kinesiology confirmed the validity of the "be patient" advice, and that it came from the redwood trees.

Love and wisdom:

Back in the chaotic years of hunger for career success and raising family, patience didn't even occur to me as an option; there were just too many urgent demands. In my retirement years, patience has found footing. Life as a writer has taught me that haste often leads to doing things over. I can now see that if I ever reach an old redwood's age, "be patient" would likely be the advice I shared with anyone who asked. Perhaps patience was always intended to be part of my personal life experience. The idea just had to be patient waiting for my trust in life to catch up!

Creation Is a Love Song

The Cosmos is eternal. Its omnipotent (all powerful), omnipresent (everywhere present), and omniscient (all knowing) nature was announced in our corner of the Cosmos when our Universe exploded into being at the Big Bang. Almost fourteen billion Earth-years later, that infinite energy field contains *everything* that exists as our Universe; one colossal presence expressing itself as its own creation.

The Universe we find ourselves within is vast beyond human comprehension, so science has yet to tell us how many dimensions exist within it, or whether there is a multiverse with many universes. But since infinity is unbounded, there are no limits to creation's possibilities. In addition, science has recently discovered that, as vast as it is, the *physical* part of the Universe represents only about *four percent* of its total energy.[xx] Science can only describe the remaining ninety-six percent as dark energy and dark matter; *dark* meaning it cannot be directly observed or measured. In truth, almost everything is non-physical! As human beings embedded within creation, that principle also applies to us. The life energy carried by our souls is vastly more than represented by our bodies.

Since everything is energy, I wonder if there really is a sharp boundary between the physical and non-physical realms. Could it be that a continuum exists based on density or vibrational frequencies of the energy comprising all the pieces of creation? Life experience suggests, and I accept as truth, that humans are a blend of body and soul; physical and non-physical. We've become fond of thinking Homo sapiens are unique in this regard, but that is a fiction of the ego. All physical creation, every last speck of it, is sustained in physical form by the non-physical creator energy within it. Everything is comprised of both spirit *and* body. My understanding of life is deeply anchored in the belief that since

God is part of every piece, all creation is inherently holy. How might our view of the world shift if we accepted *everything is holy* as our truth?

I have come to see that creation *is* a love song. It is true on the ultimate scale and equally true as each life form expresses its own creativity. It is easy to become awestruck by the *omni* words associated with the Big Bang. I don't dispute them, yet life has taught me that love and beauty are also everywhere and fundamental to everything. The beauty of dewdrops on a spider's web, or the patterns on a butterfly's wing, are obvious examples. The Bible simply states that "God is love."[xxi] Pierre Teilhard de Chardin, the prominent twentieth-century paleontologist and Jesuit brother, said, "Love is the affinity which links and draws together the elements of the world. Love, in fact, is the agent of universal synthesis."[xxii] In one of his Daily Meditations, Richard Rohr also quoted Teilhard de Chardin: "The physical structure of the universe is love."[xxiii] Indeed, the Divine Presence has been singing the ongoing music of its creation for all the eons there has been a Universe. Each fragment of creation across the entire Cosmos is continuously singing its own love song back to our common creator, just by being itself.

Creation Is a Love Song is intended to be as open-ended as the Universe, pointing the way toward the yet-to-be-revealed. I am part of creation's song; so are you. Each individual life and its pathway are anchored in love and trust by their very nature. The human ego has proven to be deeply flawed when it tries to understand and guide our walk along life's pathway. We just didn't come equipped to plan and control the mysteries of life. It took a long time for me to release the ego-illusion that control of life is even possible, let alone necessary. Surrendering my need for control has finally opened the door for life to flow in natural harmony with my soul.

Love and wisdom:

Trust your creative instinct; it's your love song calling you to sing. Each expression of creation, from a subatomic particle to the Universe, is a unique part of the divine whole. Everything, both physical and non-physical, is held within Divinity. There is no other place to be! So, it's just the nature of creation that everything belongs. There are no exceptions. Please accept that good news and sing your life song with enthusiasm and joy.

CHAPTER 3

NATURE IS THE CONTEXT FOR LIFE

"This grand show is eternal. It is always sunrise somewhere; the dew is never all dried at once; a shower is forever falling; vapor ever rising. Eternal sunrise, eternal sunset, eternal dawn and gloaming, on seas and continents and islands, each in its turn, as the round earth rolls."
— John Muir, *John of the Mountains*

With vivid precognition, John Muir described the view of Mother Earth we see in images from the International Space Station. The beautiful *grand show* has always been, is now, and will always be, the context for all life on Planet Earth. Life and planet continue to evolve together, so intricately interwoven as to be unknowable, and therefore, indescribable. Evolution of life is an ongoing process forever revealing itself over the eons. And it unfolds with a sense of direction; the evolution of life has always demonstrated a bias toward greater complexity and capability. How exciting that we are part of it!

Because creation has eternity to work with, there is no need to hurry. From a lifespan typically measured in decades, our five senses have no way to notice the rise and erosion of mountain ranges, or continental drift, or the slow unfolding of global climate change. In fact, many facets of this earthly context seem to be unchanging and timeless to us. That apparent stability brings us a sense of comfort and safety.

Love and Wisdom:

It is a marvelous blessing that human nature comes with the capacity to appreciate Mother Earth's wondrous beauty.

Wilderness

"...in Wildness is the preservation of the World"
— David Henry Thoreau, *Walking*

In late summer of a recent year, I was sitting in my car an hour west of Cody, Wyoming just inside Yellowstone National Park. With the windows and sunroof wide open, the car was filled with the scent of lodgepole pines. I found myself contemplating whether the Park, with its millions of visitors each summer, is really a wilderness. It didn't seem to be a yes or no question.

Yellowstone is a setting that leaves nature more or less alone, limited only by its popularity with tourists. The plants and animals are protected and allowed to freely move about in harmony with their own inner rhythms. The park is an enormous area, free from hunting animals or gathering plants — with one exception: fish. A Park regulation that allows trout to be gathered, released, and gathered again, is inconsistent at best; inhumane feels more accurate to me. Similarly, culling herds of animals has been deemed necessary to control populations so successful the Park's resources can no longer support their numbers. In a more enlightened world, they would be free to roam, but that's not their current reality. The reintroduction of wolves brought an enormous benefit to the balance of nature within the Park, so less culling will happen in the future.

All the millions of visitors who love Yellowstone have resulted in roads, campgrounds, hotels, restaurants, public toilets, bearproof dumpsters, gas stations, employee residences, rangers, cars, campers, trails, entrance towns, and more; all also a part of Yellowstone National Park. Because of the pressures we create, animal management is perceived to be necessary, so some of the wild ones are tracked by signals from special collars or microchips implanted under their skin. But Yellowstone is vast, so many animals are never disturbed by *management*, or the chaos at visitor facilities and along roads.

What does Yellowstone offer that calls so many to visit? What inner needs are visitors seeking to satisfy? The Park is an excellent place to see many of North America's most treasured wild creatures; beasts like bison, moose, elk, bighorn sheep, pronghorn, mule deer, grizzly bears, black bears, wolves, coyotes, lynx, bobcats, and more — all living together in dynamic balance. Without a doubt, the Park is a spectacular expression of the natural world. It is humbling to realize that most of the world was this wild only a millennium ago. The natural world has paid a heavy price for Homo sapiens' success as a species; perhaps because many of us have forgotten we are part of nature.

Many come to see Yellowstone's famous thermal features. The molten core of Mother Earth is ten times closer to the surface here than on most of the planet (three miles versus thirty miles). This provides Mother Earth with the opportunity for burping, belching, hissing, and gurgling beyond what she gets to express almost anywhere else. Sulphur emissions from many of the geysers smell like a gym full of sweaty boys, so it's not likely that tourists come for the aroma.

The ecosystem surrounding Yellowstone, including the Park itself, is a wilderness of roughly thirteen million acres; easily the largest in the United States outside of Alaska. The beauty of the region's rivers also draw people to Yellowstone. If you walk far enough upstream along any major river in this region, except the Jefferson, you will find yourself in Yellowstone National Park. Its high plateau and mountains spawn an array of rivers that are justly famous for their beauty, waterfalls, whitewater rapids, and trout fishing.

With all its iconic wildlife, it might seem odd that, for me, a fish would come to symbolize the uniqueness of the great wilderness that is Yellowstone National Park. The Yellowstone cutthroat trout is a sub-species native only to the region of North America in and surrounding Yellowstone; primarily in its namesake river and upper portion of the Snake River. Its coloration is similar to other cutthroats, with the typical distinct slash of bright orange color along its lower jaw back to its gill cover. The dark spots toward its tail are large enough to distinguish it from other cutthroats. Its overall coloration features less pink than other cutthroats, so copper and gold shades are more prevalent. But they are far from bland, as the red around its face and gold elsewhere become more prominent during spawning season. Even today, a thirty-inch-plus specimen is occasionally landed by a fortunate angler.

I have always tended to root for the underdog, which might be why I see the Yellowstone cutthroat as a fitting symbol. Compared to Yellowstone's other wildlife, it seems more vulnerable to being lost as a distinct expression of nature's creative genius. The range of genetically pure Yellowstone cutthroats has shrunk to only five percent for many reasons; particularly overfishing and stocking of non-native trout — rainbow trout readily interbreed with cutthroats, and introduced lake trout are voracious predators of smaller cutthroats in their natural stronghold of Yellowstone Lake. Most of the remaining genetically pure Yellowstone cutthroat trout are found within the Park boundaries. Sadly, but not surprising, humankind's old habit of tinkering with nature has intruded deep into the heart of Yellowstone country.

Because I love rivers, I will give a brief review of those that originate in Yellowstone. Beginning in West Yellowstone, Montana and moving clockwise one first encounters the Madison River, born at the confluence of the Gibbon and Firehole Rivers within the Park at Madison Junction. Thus begins one of the premier trout streams in the world, often rated number one in the contiguous forty-eight states. It flows west and then north along the Madison Mountain Range toward Three Forks, Montana. On the east side of the same mountains, the Gallatin River flows north from the Park's northwest corner, also headed for Three Forks. The Gallatin is smaller than the Madison, but perhaps even more scenic, flowing through its beautiful canyon past the ski resort at Big Sky, Montana. This is where some of the classic fishing scenes were filmed for the movie, *A River Runs Through It*.

These two rivers combine with the Jefferson River at Three Forks to form the Missouri River, headwaters of North America's great river system. The Jefferson drains the east side of the Continental Divide west of Yellowstone down to Three Forks. If, like me, you know water to be the lifeblood of Mother Earth, or are interested in how the geography of rivers shapes the flow of human migrations and the history of nations, then Three Forks, Montana is sacred ground. The Jefferson and Madison join first to form the Missouri, which is then joined by the Gallatin a few hundred yards downstream. Three Forks doesn't look much different from the rest of the valley, but it is a singular location in the whole of North America.

The waters of Yellowstone Lake, in the heart of the Park, are unique in all the world — remarkably pure since there are no sources of manmade pollution anywhere upstream. The lake is also infused with high levels of minerals and Earth energy from the hundreds of thermal vents that contribute to its makeup. The Yellowstone River begins as the outlet from this extraordinary lake. By the time it exits the Park via its northern boundary at Gardiner, Montana, it is already a master stream that dominates southern Montana's landscape. The Missouri River has already accumulated six major dams by the time it reaches their confluence in South Dakota. In comparison, the Yellowstone's six-hundred-seventy-mile length makes it the longest undammed river in the contiguous forty-eight states — something of a miracle for a major river running through the irrigation-thirsty American west. I like to think its waters are so sacred that they simply refused to ever be dammed. My heart knows the Yellowstone River is a symbol of freedom that must remain unfettered for as long as it flows!

The Clark's Fork of the Yellowstone River exits the Park near its northeast corner and joins the rest of the Yellowstone southwest of Billings, Montana. It cuts a dramatic canyon through the Absaroka Mountains northwest of Cody, Wyoming. The Clark's Fork is believed to be the escape route taken by Chief Joseph and his band of Nimiipuu in their bold dash from reservation life in Idaho toward freedom in Canada. My reverence for freedom makes it seem sad that the US cavalry caught up with them only a few miles south of the border.

The east-facing side of the Absaroka Range and Yellowstone Park are drained by the North and South Forks of the Shoshone River. The Shoshone created some rugged country cutting its way to combine with the Wind River in northern Wyoming. Their confluence is now beneath Bighorn Lake formed behind Yellowtail Dam. From there the Bighorn River flows northeast to join the Yellowstone at Bighorn, Montana. All of the rivers noted so far drain the northeast side of the Continental Divide that cuts a diagonal through the Park.

The entire southwestern slope of Yellowstone is drained by the Snake River and its tributaries. The main branch flows south along the spectacular mountains of Grand Teton National Park, before turning west around the south end of the range to enter southern Idaho. The Henry's Fork of the Snake River drains the west side of the Continental Divide, south of West Yellowstone, to join the rest of the Snake near Rexburg, Idaho. The Snake flows further west to join the mighty Columbia River near Pasco in south-central Washington. It deeply anchors my love for Yellowstone country that its pristine waters display such beauty and freedom and bless so much of our nation.

Just inside the Park on a Tuesday evening heading back to Cody, and again in the same area on the following Thursday morning drive into Yellowstone, a big old silverback grizzly crossed the road in front of me. It was interesting that he avoided looking at me or my car, so I never saw his face. His coat was a dark shaggy brown, shading into silver gray along his spine. He must have weighed several hundred pounds; large enough to see his back through the side window as he walked right alongside the passenger side of my SUV. He carried himself with confidence borne of his position as the dominant creature in his part of Yellowstone. His sex was in obvious view between his back legs as he walked across the road toward the sheltering forest. Although his pace was brisk as he moved away from me, I sensed no fear in him, just his natural uneasiness with cars, and the carnival atmosphere that gathers along Yellowstone's roadways when he is visible. I managed a couple of mediocre pictures to prove I didn't hallucinate the great beast. It was a privilege just to see him; especially in this wilderness setting. Even though he was outfitted with a well-worn tracking collar, this bear's demeanor would never be confused with that of a zoo animal. It made me sad for his imprisoned relatives.

Later that Thursday afternoon, I was sitting at a picnic table more than thirty miles east of the Park along the North Fork of the Shoshone River. A sign along the road and the warning attached to the table told me I was still in grizzly country, so it is obvious that the Yellowstone ecosystem extends far beyond the formal Park boundary. There is a Nature Conservancy preserve even further east toward Cody that protects a favored grizzly denning area. Along with its rivers, the fact that wild grizzly bears live here in unfettered freedom also speaks volumes about what Yellowstone is, and what it means to me.

Love and wisdom:

Yellowstone Park's boundary does not exist in the knowing of our wild brothers and sisters. Our responsibility, as stewards of Mother Earth, is to honor the wild creatures' inner map and wisdom of where they need to be. To do otherwise is abdication of our duty as the planet's caretakers. Everything is a sacred expression of divine creation, and we are called to open our hearts to the entire family of life.

The Shoshone canyon west of Cody is similar to many large canyons where the inner hills and ridges block one's view of the outer ridgelines high above and beyond the inner canyon. Such canyons are a good metaphor for life; there is always more present than we can see from where we stand.

For years I have tried to understand my lifelong obsession to be in wild nature. I call it an obsession because I often feel restless whenever I am away from it. A few years ago, wisdom came that contentment would remain elusive so long as I thought of wilderness as external and separate from me. Wilderness is not only *out there*, it is *in here*. In unspoiled nature I feel the song of the wild, and the untamed part of me sings in harmony. I am part of its rhythms and seasons, one with all of its creatures. I am the granite canyon and the river that cuts its way to freedom. I am wilderness and it is me. Yellowstone inspires hope that together we can create a world where all life thrives in *inter*dependent freedom. What a magnificent possibility!

Water

"Water is the driving force of all nature."
— Leonardo da Vinci

The several rivers that originate in Yellowstone are even more meaningful in light of the sacred nature of water itself. Dr. Masuro Emoto's fascinating work reported in his book, *The Secret Life of Water,* has shown that the structure of water responds to our emotions by changing to be in harmony with our feelings.[xxiv] When our emotion is love, freezing water forms beautiful symmetrical crystal patterns; when it feels anger, hate, or other negative emotions, the crystals are distorted with no beautiful patterns at all. The ice crystals formed as water is frozen can indeed reflect the consciousness it has absorbed from those in its proximity. It reminds me of Pierre Teilhard de Chardin's assertion that the very structure of the Universe is love. When you know this, it seems natural to feel gratitude for every swallow of water you drink.

I first became aware of treating water with reverence when reading Tom Brown, Jr's book, *Grandfather*. The book tells about the author's training in ancient Earth wisdom as a child. His mentor was an old Apache shaman named Stalking Wolf, grandfather of his best friend and fellow student. Whenever Stalking Wolf put his hand in a river or pond to drink, he always paused to express his gratitude to all the waters of the world before he drank.[xxv]

Even in wilderness areas, drinking unfiltered water might seem unwise in the twenty-first century. So, I have modified Grandfather's blessing ceremony and use it often. For many years, whenever I am moved by the beauty of a lake or river, or pump drinking water from any natural source while hiking, I take a moment to place my hand in the water to let it feel my gratitude. Then I speak aloud my thanks to the water for what it is and what it means to life. The words are inspired by, and naturally flow from, the awe I am feeling at that moment. It is always spontaneous, so there is no specific form or set of words for this ritual. In some fashion, I always speak gratitude to the water for its beauty and for its role as the sustainer of life. It is both the soother of my soul and the circulatory system of Mother Earth. By this point in my life, I harbor no doubt that water is sacred and holy. When I am in the presence of a free-flowing wild river, feeling gratitude in my body and reverence in my heart is as natural as breathing. The ceremony always ends with "Amen."

I have been blessed by many dozens of rivers and lakes through this ceremony over the years, yet there remains a sense of untapped potential in my relationship with water. I aspire to feel the unfettered joy seen in the face of a friend emerging after a long moment of self-baptism in India's Ganges River. On many occasions, reverence has been felt with my hand immersed in natural waters to express my gratitude. The waters of choice have often been icy cold mountain streams, so my ritual must often end before I'm ready. Full body immersion seems outrageous! Intuition suggests these connections would be stronger if they were more complete or lasted longer. Nonetheless, Stalking Wolf's ceremony has been a meaningful practice.

Curiosity led me to use applied kinesiology to better understand water. Surprisingly, my results disagreed with Dr. Emoto's conclusions drawn from his observations. He interpreted water's ability to respond to his experiments as an indication that water has its own consciousness. AK indicated water does *not* carry its own consciousness (i.e., it is not aware of itself). Remarkably, however, AK confirmed that water has the capacity to sense and to mirror back to us *our* emotions, words, thoughts, and even our prayers.

Water also happens to be the most important substance on Planet Earth; so essential that life as we know it cannot exist without it. To emphasize the point, on average, water makes up 57-60 percent of our body weight. Oxygen is also vital for many life forms, but not universally required. Anerobic bacteria exist without it, even in your own gut. There also are deep sea creatures living near volcanic vents in the ocean's depths, that thrive via chemistry based on sulphur, rather than oxygen. But nowhere on Earth does life exist in the long-term absence of water. Given life's need for water, it is natural to see all the waters of Mother Earth as her circulatory system. Nature's hydrologic cycle purifies it via evaporation and is the pump (heart) that circulates it. There is undeniable creative energy on this planet, and much of it is carried by water. No wonder anthropologist and nature writer Loren Eiseley said, "If there is magic on this planet, it is contained in water." [xxvi]

Mountains

"Climb the mountains and get their good tidings. Nature's peace will flow into you as sunshine flows into trees. The winds will blow their own freshness into you, and the storms their energy, while cares will drop away from you like autumn leaves."
— John Muir, *Our National Parks*

Our bodies tell us that hiking around in the mountains can be really hard work, yet millions of people love to do just that whenever they can. John Muir's quote explains why, and experience allows me to bear witness to its truth. Mountains are more than spectacular scenery. Their powerful presence grounds me to the land in mysterious ways I find hard to describe. To say I love the mountains doesn't quite fit, yet they feel almost like family — something like a distant cousin I don't know very well. I love how mountains humble and inspire me at the same time.

A key point of my relationship with mountains is how they have facilitated spiritual growth and inner peace. The Andes and the Himalayas are the highest mountain ranges on Earth, but that is only part of their appeal. Being in the presence of Mt. Veronica in Peru and Jhomolhari and Jichu Drake in Bhutan moved me deeply. But only two mountains on Earth felt like they were my children; it happened when I met Stok Kangri and Kangyaze in the Stok Range of the Himalayas of northwest India. That Ladakh trek in 2005 opened the most epic jolt of spiritual growth experienced in this lifetime. It is difficult to describe and impossible to overstate the flow of blessings that have come since those soul-expanding experiences. Although Ladakh was an apex of my life, that story has been told in *The Great University of Life* and is too long to repeat here. [xxvii] It is sufficient to say that my perceptions were blown wide open to reveal understandings of soul life and reincarnation that I had never before imagined. I learned that my soul has had hundreds of prior earthly lives over nearly 75,000 Earth-years, including two in the Indus River valley in Ladakh where our trek began. Applied kinesiology was essential for confidence that the infusion of new information was actually reliable and true.

The subsistence herdsmen and farmers that live in isolated Himalayan and Andean villages carry an uncommon openness and grace, as if life in the mountains left no room for pretentions.

Perhaps the majesty and harshness of mountain life, coupled with their deeply anchored oneness with the land, helps them embrace both *inter*dependence and humility. Being in their presence feels peaceful and authentic. One instinctively trusts them. The freedom of heart and mind encountered in Ladakh remarkably expanded my understanding of life's context and meaning. It felt miraculous at the time, and the experiences still inspire me many years later. I am forever grateful!

Mountains have shaped my life in other ways. They were calling me to Colorado in my mid-teens, long before the doors finally opened to move here over forty years ago. Even now it's hard to describe, but I was emotionally attached to the Colorado Rockies long before I ever saw them in person. They were an archetype representing wild unspoiled nature that my heart knew was deeply important for me to experience. When I witness how my life has unfolded, moving here was a keystone for my soul over this entire lifetime as Foster. Moving to Colorado has never disappointed me and I have never grown tired of her mountains. From the moment that it arose in my awareness, my soul would not let me forget the call to live in Colorado until I finally moved here after twenty-plus years of yearning. The relationship with her mountains, and the expanded life I found here, have since shifted to ever-deepening gratitude.

Yet, even though I have hiked thousands of miles all over them, communing with Colorado's mountains feels different than my experiences in the Andes and Himalayas. I think it's the people, more than the mountains. People in first world mountain towns, with their wealth of ski resorts, recreational amenities, shops, and tourist venues seem distracted from the land and their own essential nature, compared to subsistence herders and farmers — or so it feels when I come down from the trails.

For me, the most physically impressive mountain on Earth is Denali, sheltered in the center of Denali National Park and Preserve in Alaska. The name Denali simply means "the tall one," as she has always been called by the Koyukuk tribe who live to her north along the Yukon River that carries their name. While many peaks in the Himalayas and Karakoram, along with several in the Andes, top out higher above sea level, Denali is as regal in every way. In terms of the view from base to top, she is the tallest mountain on Earth. Mt. Kilimanjaro in Tanzania is second. It's true that Hawaii's Big Island has two peaks, Mauna Loa and Mauna Kea, that are taller from base to top, but their bases are seventeen thousand feet down on the ocean floor, so there is no view from base to top. Denali is so impressive due to her enormous presence within her native landscape. From a hundred miles away, she still completely dominates the horizon. Unlike the Himalayas or Andes, there are no nearby mountains even close to her magnitude, so she stands virtually alone, dwarfing all her neighbors. Perhaps she is also compelling because she seems so reluctant to be seen at all. She is consistently lost in her own cloudy swirl of weather created by altitude, size, and her far north location. Her upper regions are a place of eternal winter. Many people visit Denali National Park and never see her at all.

Although Denali is in a first world nation, both the Park and her mountain centerpiece are isolated from the noise and confusion of life as a tourist attraction; all that is a hundred miles away at the park entrance. The difficulty of getting to Denali, and the rigors of exploring it, limit close experience of her to expert, well-prepared outdoor enthusiasts. In addition, no-one lives nearby, because it is isolated in the midst of a six-million-acre Park. There is only one ninety-mile road in Denali Park from the entrance to four wilderness lodges deep in its interior. It is unpaved after the first several miles, and private vehicles are not allowed. Guests must ride tour buses operated by the National Park Service. To put this isolation in perspective, Denali National Park and Preserve is the size of Massachusetts with one ninety mile, mostly unpaved road, that is not open to private cars — and Denali has no permanent human residents.

Our visit to Denali in 2015 felt like a pilgrimage. Our first day in the Park was mesmerizing because we saw so many animals. The bus driver/guide said we were seeing more grizzly bears and moose than any other day all summer. But Denali herself teased us all day with only faint glimpses of lower slopes through her clouds. Our second day we explored the Alaska Range with a helicopter tour and glacier landing. The morning was delightfully clear but the helicopter took us into the Alaska Range away from Denali, so she was behind us out of sight. It made us wish helicopters came with rear-view mirrors! Fortunately, the remote mountain scenery, Dall sheep sightings, and the rivers of ice, helped us forget what we might be missing. The glacier landing and walk was a unique experience for all of us. The Alaska Range helped me imagine how Colorado's mountains looked several millennia ago when they were similarly ice-covered.

The flight back to the landing pad was breath-taking. Denali stood bright and enormous far above her smaller sisters; not a cloud in the sky. Our pilot said this was the best day of the entire summer to see Denali. The train ride back to Anchorage that afternoon continued the dream. Denali was with us all day against a vibrant blue sky; the train even made photo stops at several superb viewing points. It was a glorious day to be in the unique presence of Earth's most dominant mountain.

Love and wisdom:

One is left to ponder the power and meaning mountains hold. A virgin forest, the seashore with brisk winds to showcase the ocean's power, and the vastness of remote prairies or deserts evoke similar feelings of awe and unfettered oneness with creation; but it's no accident that I have chosen life next to Colorado's mountains. All these realms of unspoiled nature make it clear that life's drama and distractions are not as urgent as they seem. The only thing required to feel the peace of these realms is taking time to notice.

Prairies

"Anyone can love the mountains, but it takes a soul to love the prairie."
— Willa Cather

Prairies are by definition a natural grassland. They have few trees because sparse average rainfall gives grasses the upper hand. My favorite grassland in the world is Serengeti National Park in Tanzania, East Africa. It is big enough, and was preserved soon enough, so that its natural predator/prey populations remain in sufficient numbers and balance to be self-sustaining into the twenty-first century. To know one is in wild country it is only necessary to step a few yards away from the safari vehicle. You will quickly be alert and aware; each step away from the vehicle is a step into a world where you are nowhere near the top of the food chain. Hiking in grizzly country has a similar effect on one's alertness.

America's *Serengeti National Park*[7] could have been as extraordinary, but it never happened. Our ancestors were less than fifty years too late. The land and the animals were present for millennia, but our nation was too young and preoccupied with more urgent priorities like slavery, our Civil War, and the *Indian problem*. As the old saying goes, timing is everything. Long before Europeans arrived, climate shifts associated with the end of the last ice age, coupled with predation by native hunters, had pushed many megafauna species (mammoths, mastodons, giant bison, giant short-faced bears, saber-tooth tigers, etc.), as well as the American horse, into the abyss of extinction. But the vast prairies of North America were still worthy of designation as *America's Serengeti* well into the nineteenth century. In their free-ranging days before our nation's

---

7   A term used by Dan Flores in his book *American Serengeti: The Last Big Animals of the Great Plains*

Euro-American westward expansion, bison, elk, deer, wolves, grizzlies, cougars, and many smaller animals roamed the entire vast heartland of North America from the Rocky Mountains to the Appalachians, and from Texas to southern Canada.

Before Colorado became home, I lived for a decade in Elk County, (western) Pennsylvania; so-named because elk once lived there. With a tip of the hat to nostalgia, it's delightful that a small herd was reintroduced there nearly a hundred years ago. It now is reported to number close to a thousand animals, but I never saw a wild elk until I moved west.

When Yellowstone, the first National Park in the world, was established in 1872, bison were on the verge of extinction, with only a few dozen animals scattered across vast distances. Their predators retreated with them to the Rocky Mountains in search of safety and food. The last few bison left in the remote backcountry of Yellowstone, along with a few stragglers in Alberta and Manitoba, became the ancestors of the half million or so that live today in North America. Yellowstone National Park was created just in time! At the time, the primary interest was protecting her remarkable thermal features, but my heart sings that the iconic animals were part of the package.

As Willa Cather's quote implies, the beauty of native prairies is subtler. Their vast expanses of open grasslands with unbounded views fading to hazy horizons leave one feeling humble and exposed. Animals, including humans, require food, water, and shelter to survive. To many twenty-first century humans, none of these things seem obvious on natural prairie. The skies are enormous with weather to match. Winter blizzards and summer dust storms, tornados, and thunderstorms occasionally snatch life from an unprepared or unlucky person, as easily as not waking up in the morning.

But, one can feel the breath of the Universe in the rhythm of prairies. As Ms. Cather implied, prairies touch my soul differently than mountain grandeur. My instincts say prairies provide a more expansive context for life. Being part of a wagon train from St. Louis to Oregon must have felt something akin to rowing an outrigger canoe across the 1500 miles of open ocean between Tahiti and Hawaii. The pioneers faced a vast sea of grass with dangers imagined and real between them and the *land of promise* they were seeking. Prairies feel too unbounded and exposed to be comfortable; they go on and on with almost no place to hide from the unexpected.

One can see crossing the prairies as a metaphor for one's spiritual journey. Life can buffet us with the yin and yang of challenges and rewards not anticipated or even imagined. Similarly, our spiritual journey offers us no place to hide from God or self when the pathway enters strange and foreboding territory. As with mountains, I love how prairies inspire and humble me at the same time. Their power would be more obvious had a vast swath of North America's Serengeti actually been preserved.

The Gypsum Hills

I am blessed to know a place where one can feel what that American Serengeti might have been like. My wife's hometown is Medicine Lodge, in south-central Kansas. It sits along the Medicine River at the east edge of a raised tableland called the Gypsum Hills. Once the territory of the Kiowa Indians, the hills cover something like fifteen hundred square miles, an island of cedar, creeks, and canyons in what was once a vast sea of prairie. The main drainage from the hills is the mineral-laden Medicine River, held sacred by the Kiowa because of its water's healing powers. A medicine lodge, at the confluence of the river and Elm Creek, was honored as a place free from intertribal conflict by all five southern plains tribes, because access to the healing waters was so important.

It was natural that this peaceful location was chosen by the southern plains tribes as the site to sign a peace treaty with the US government in 1867. Although the treaty's effectiveness was short-lived, its intent is still commemorated in Medicine Lodge with a Peace Treaty Pageant historical reenactment every three to four years.[xxviii] Native descendants of the original signers of the treaty document participate along with the town's residents, so it has an air of authenticity that would otherwise be missing. Although the event is mostly known in Kansas and Oklahoma, the peace and cooperation it symbolizes are calling all humanity to wake up and listen. The land and waters in these hills are still as sacred as the American Indians knew them to be. The *Gyp* Hills would have been the perfect centerpiece for America's Serengeti National Park.

Natural Patience

"...adopt the pace of nature; her secret is patience."
— Ralph Waldo Emerson, *Complete Words: Volume X*

It is early May 2014 and the Gypsum Hills are drier than most anyone can remember. Just when they should be green to the horizon, most everything remains brown. Subtle details of their contours are revealed by wisps of green in areas lying just a bit lower than their surroundings. The extra moisture where snow collected in modest depressions during the dry winter helped the grasses barely shake off their dormancy. Wildflowers are also late and scarce. There might be just enough time for a late burst of spring if rains come soon, but the ten-day forecast says it will remain hot and dry. The beauty of spring in the Gypsum Hills will be a nostalgic memory again this year; the fourth dry year in a row for much of Kansas and the western United States. These are hard times to be a rancher in the Gypsum Hills. Some have sold their cattle, for lack of grass and cash to buy hay from faraway places with more rain or irrigated fields.

In the first half of this morning, I spotted only three swallows, a single black beetle, and a couple of scrawny flies. Later, I would see some scattered clumps of wildflowers, many tiny butterflies concentrated with the flowers, and a pair of whitetail deer. When I was patient and listened to the hills more closely, the good news was revealed. The grass, flowers, and animals have developed tenacity and patience to cope with erratic weather. Some May, when the rains come, the Gypsum Hills will be green with grass and graced by fragrant wildflowers in abundance. In the meanwhile, all of us who care have no choice but to wait with them.

Two more years: After several years of dry weather, 2015 brought the long-awaited wet spring. The drought did not compromise at all the capacity of the Gypsum Hills to bring forth their natural abundance when the rains came. The hills and ranchers celebrated the grass and flowers with those who love beauty. When we are struggling through the dry spells that life sometimes brings, it might help to remember nature's patience — and its exuberance when it is rewarded. The delight of spring, 2015 brought hope that it would herald a trend of weather more aligned with our desires, but it might also be an aberration of a new normal. Either way, the natural patience of the Gypsum Hills will be tested again in future years. All of nature shares the common ground of life's inevitable cycles.

2016 brought another very dry spring. The exuberant growth from the prior year dried into explosively flammable tinder. The grasslands celebrated the spring equinox with the largest wildfire on private land in our nation's history. It burned over four-hundred-sixty square miles; nearly three hundred-thousand acres. No human life was lost, but wild animals, cattle, ranch buildings, equipment, and many miles of fence lines were destroyed. Just two weeks later rains came and the grasses exploded back to life, nourished by the ashes.

Love and wisdom:

Even fire can bless the prairie's natural resilience. By Thanksgiving of 2016, a golden sheen of ripe grass again covered the hills. Only scorched trees remained to remember the great fire. Just so, we humans have the opportunity emerge from life's apparent disasters to find new inspiration, growth, and joy.

Then and Now

"Geology gives us a key to the patience of God."
— Josiah Gilbert Holland

The air is cool this morning in the Gypsum Hills, but the sun carries surprising warmth as the winter solstice approaches. In an ancient time, the scene before me was a brackish seabed, part of North America's great inland sea. Water carried iron-bearing silt from surrounding mountains that was interlayered with deposits of the mineral gypsum, left when the sea evaporated during long dry spells. Many such cycles resulted in layer upon layer of red sandstone and white gypsum slowly building during the Cretaceous Era. Eventually, the land rose and the sea's bottom dried. It has taken eighty-million years of slow-motion changes to rearrange that ancient seabed into the radiant flat-topped hills and canyons that lie before me.

A century lifespan is unusually long for a human. It was eight-hundred-thousand centuries ago when the ancient seabed began to rise, signaling its end. It's beyond human capacity — our species arrived on the world stage only two-thousand centuries ago — to imagine that sweep of time.

As I sat immersed in the scene, the light shining from the Gypsum Hills seemed to originate deeper than the sunlight reflecting from their surfaces. Just as there is much more to a person than the surface we can see, it is obvious here today that Mother Earth is much more than we typically perceive. As if to affirm that thought, a small hawk just flew across my view. Its belly, chest, and the underside of its wings were cream colored, while its head, upper body, and the top of its wings were slate gray. It was too large for a kestrel, but still a small hawk. Its overall shape and size, flying motion, colors, and speed said it was a peregrine falcon. I have rarely seen them in Colorado, and never expected to see one in Kansas. What a treat!

My heart wants to better know this land I am communing with. I wish to walk on it, admire the views, and peer into its cedar-choked gulleys and brushy bottom lands, while meandering its mesa edges. It would hold deep meaning to float down the sacred waters of the Medicine River on a tranquil summer evening as its healing waters soothed my aging bones. Today it is not easy to follow such longings. There are fences everywhere and *keep out* signs are common. The river's flow is low and streambed activities sometimes leave it muddy. Since the Peace Treaty year of 1867, the sacred heritage of the river has been much compromised.

Sitting in the comfort of my modern auto, it was challenging to imagine this scene as it was only two hundred years ago. Back then, there would have been no fences, roads, traffic, highway signs, plowed fields, cattle ponds, ranch buildings, oil wells, storage tanks, and associated paraphernalia. The sounds that came to my ears and smells that found my nose would not have included autos, oil production, fertilizers, herbicides, and pesticides, along with cattle feed lots. Last evening's beautiful sunset had a dozen jet contrails crisscrossing through it. Two centuries ago, nature's beauty was not required to accommodate them.

If I was a Kiowa warrior sitting on my horse contemplating these same hills in the early 1800s, there would also be many things that are similar to the view from my car. The contours of the horizon would be familiar and the breeze on my face would feel the same. But the sounds and odors carried by the wind would bring nothing *unnatural*. I would feel at home with the land, the sky, and weather. The hills, streams, and valleys would have been home for my people for many generations. No-one owned the land, so there were no fences. These hills had always been our home, so there was no need for roads to faraway places. The reasons for many things that seem essential in the twenty-first century would have been absent from my thinking.

This land has intimately known creatures that have not walked here for decades. Not far back in time, these hills were a complete ecosystem holding bears, cougars, wolves, and smaller carnivores, in natural balance with bison, elk, deer, and smaller prey animals. In the twenty-first century, many people live isolated from nature. But the native people who knew these hills as home were immersed in nature and knew they were part of it. Just two-hundred years ago these hills really were a modest corner in America's vast Serengeti.

Love and wisdom:

Sitting here today I know this land and its waters remain as sacred as they have ever been. Although the Gypsum Hills are unique in their particular ways, all ground everywhere in the Cosmos is holy. The energy of creation is everywhere on Planet Earth, eternally humming away, often just beneath the edges of human perception. It is time for all of us to reclaim our reverence for Mother Earth as a sacred expression of divine love.

Yes, and ...

"In my Father's house are many mansions, ..."
John 14:2, KJV

My understanding of nature as the context for life has greatly expanded over the past few years. I now believe nature is the context for all life across the entire Cosmos. This expanded perception took hold when Richard Rohr blessed me with the concept of "yes, and..." thinking.[8] Until I accepted "yes, and..." my mental processes had been trapped in "either/or" thinking. My training as a scientist taught me to question everything. I really needed to understand *how* a new viewpoint related to the existing one, and *whether* the new one would be superior. Those *how* and *whether* questions were a trusted tool of the scientist I was from college until retirement.

---

8   Richard Rohr, *Yes, and ...: Daily Meditations*

Now, two decades into retirement, it is finally clear that my overly analytical approach had been out of balance with my soul's intentions. I came into this life to experience an ever-expanding love relationship with life and Divinity, but despite that, resistance to change often prevailed. Holding the paradox that two divergent views could both be valid was not part of my mental process for decades. My ego was also a big factor in resisting changes in my beliefs; it feared being wrong.

The example that broke through into an expanded "yes, and..." view of reality involved two dramatically different views of soul life. Over the past few years, I had accepted the work of Michael Newton, PhD, a hypnotherapist who spent most of his career regressing people into the spiritual realms between earthly incarnations. He was thorough and very organized in documenting his therapy sessions with several thousand clients. Their descriptions of life in the realm of souls were consistent, and a logical extension of the religious beliefs I had carried since childhood. My old ideas didn't have to be tossed out; just relaxed enough to expand. That made it easier to allow Newton's teachings to enlarge my truth.

Then, over a six-month period, our spiritual book club read three books by Machaelle Small Wright.[9] They tell the story of how her life evolved in extraordinary ways to include many elements well beyond what had been her (and my) more conventional beliefs. Her extra-normal life alternated daily between two lives

---

9   *Perelandra Garden Workbook, Behaving as if the God in All Life Mattered, Dancing in the Shadows of the Moon*

in two bodies, one located on Earth and the other on a parallel earth-like planet within our Universe. Her soul switched between the two bodies like it was changing its clothes. Although they feel *close-by* to her, the two planets exist in distinctly separate physical dimensions and realities. Like Michael Newton, Ms. Wright provided detailed explanations of her life experiences and how it all works. She has learned to control movements of energy by remarkable methods, communicated with nature entities about her garden, and found herself working with extraterrestrial beings that have the capacity for interstellar travel across the Universe. To read all this about a woman who is also an ordinary gardener like me and call it *mind-stretching* would be a masterful understatement. I was incredulous.

At the same time, my inner knowing resonated with *both* Wright and Newton. Yet, their understanding of soul life is vastly different, so this retired scientist — still stuck in either/or thinking — assumed one of them had to be *right*. But there was also certainty in my mind that the infinite nature of Divinity held room to hold both views in its reality. Finally accepting that both Wright and Newton could hold valid viewpoints is a great example of "yes, and..." thinking. This whole experience made it clear that when I have *no way* to know whether one point of view is better than another, I really *don't need* to know. When I looked at *Newton vs. Wright* in this way, the need to decide who was right simply evaporated.

Love and wisdom:

In truth, it is far more important and feasible for humans to trust life than to understand it. While Machaelle Small Wright's life may sound like fantasy to many people whose lives seem solidly earth-bound, there is no question that the inspiration and wisdom of love infuse the entire Cosmos, including each of our daily lives. While this is eternally true for each of us, our soul's incarnated sojourns are meant to be shaped and focused by those human experiences. That's why we chose to come here.

CHAPTER 4

CREATION AND HUMANITY

"Humankind, full of all creative possibilities, is God's work. Humankind alone is called to assist God. Humankind is called to co-create."
— Hildegard of Bingen

As part of creation, our earthly lives are anchored in the infinity of God. As a result, I *am* love; so are you. Yet, at the same time we are undeniably human. This is a beautiful example of a "yes, and ..." truth. We are always a blend of both human and divine (body and soul) at every moment of earthly life — it's inescapable.

It is easy to feel awe when viewing the beauty of the Cosmos through modern telescopes. Similarly, microscopes have revealed a universe of wonder and grandeur within each body. The infinite creative genius of God is obvious whenever we give it our attention. Expressing our creativity and sharing beauty bring joy and meaning to life. Because we are literally part of God, held within its eternal essence, it must be true that God inspires our creativity and feels our joy as we express it. But, I think, Hildegard's quote is too limiting when it says humans alone are called to co-create with God. Each facet of creation co-creates with God just by expressing its gifts. What is different about God inspiring a writer or scientist as compared to a spider or a bird? Do not the design of the spider's web or the bluebird's nest originate within the same infinite God as Leonardo's Mona Lisa or this book? Is the fruit of plants any less creative a gift to the world than the lives of the animal kingdom? All creation arose within God, so everything is part of that sacred energy. Only the human ego thinks our lives and creativity are somehow elevated above other parts of creation. A human could no more spin a spider's web than a spider could write a symphony — and neither we nor spiders can grow strawberries from our abdomen. Within God there are no favorites and no hierarchy. *Everything* in creation is a sacred gift rooted in God's divine love.

The Great Mystery — Another Name for God

"The ways of creation are wrapt in mystery. We
may only marvel, and bow our head."
— Albert Einstein

Most adults would say their understanding of God has grown and changed over time. When I was a small boy, my perception of God was a powerful, not very friendly, always watching me, judge in the sky. As life matured me from then until now, impressions have expanded and become less certain; much harder to grasp and describe. The old adage seems to apply; "the more I learn, the less I know." Well along in my senior years, I have come to see God as an *infinite presence* that includes all creation, both physical and non-physical, as well as the intelligence and volition behind creation. We humans refer to this ultimate infinity using whatever word carries the meaning *God* across the many languages found on Earth. In truth, human understanding of the word *God* reflects the variety of people who are pondering it. Inconsistency is unavoidable because human understanding of God can only be partial; God's infinite nature and essence lie way beyond our finite human capacities. A current summary of my personal belief: I see God as the loving volition, intelligence, and energy comprising all creation. I *know* I am part of that energy.

Because God is infinite, it makes sense to me that there is no *other* place where creation could have arisen. And everything must exist within it. The infinite nature of God also means our *finite* human condition is hopelessly inadequate to grasp its nature. That's okay; if life required us to comprehend the nature of God, we would know it — or we wouldn't be here. God is *The Great Mystery*. Life flows much more smoothly when we accept that mystery and learn to trust God in spite of it.

Yet, despite its omnipotent mystery, God is no stranger. Because creation originated within God and its one infinite energy field comprises all that is, you can see God just by looking around. Anything in your surroundings, no matter where your gaze falls, *is part of God*, including the next person you see, even the one in your mirror. Your essential nature is this: *you are God* in miniature. The only difference is one of scale, not essence. This is not an ego trip, and we are not unique. Every facet of creation innately holds the right to bow and say, "Namaste" to everything else; "the divine in me honors the divine in you."

Science is a methodology developed by humanity over the past few millennia. I have a graduate degree in materials science, so it is natural that many books, read over much of my life, have informed this short summary on science. Two that especially expanded my belief system are Primack and Abrams, *The View from the Center of the Universe* and Brian Green's, *The Elegant Universe*. For a writer it's disappointing, but there is no way to trace the source for every facet of my current belief system, or how it all came together. That is likely true for everyone.

There is nothing about science that is inherently out of harmony with, or in competition with, God or religion. Science can be seen as humanity's efforts to understand, and make use of, the natural laws that govern how creation operates. The scientific method uses experiments and mathematics to learn and describe how nature behaves. Science is fundamentally similar to theology. Although they use very different tools, both are approaching the same Great Mystery. In that sense, both can be seen as efforts to know God. Science and religion have both penetrated with deeper understanding the near edges of The Great Mystery, but their work will never be complete. God is infinite.

The General Theory of Relativity, developed by Albert Einstein, does a great job of aligning with and predicting the behavior of the

Universe on a grand scale. The mathematics Einstein developed to express that theory require a beginning point in time. Science has also shown that the physical Universe has been expanding ever since its beginning. This ongoing expansion implies a point of origin if one imagines that process in reverse. These two factors led to general acceptance that there must have been a Big Bang when the Universe began.

That point of origin in space/time could be thought of mathematically as the ultimate singularity; to me it feels like the energy of God waiting to express itself as the Universe. That idea carries the implication that, an instant before the Big Bang, there was no Universe; nothing physical at all — only unmanifested potential awaiting its release. That begs the question, "What and where were the vast energies of the Universe before it emerged?" I wonder whether humanity has the capacity to answer this question.

Our current favored story about the Universe proclaims that around 13.8 billion Earth-years ago, the great singularity, "God in waiting," literally exploded as a ball of churning energy; an entire universe in the making. At that incredible instant, when time began and everything seemed to emerge from nothing, the Great Mystery declared its presence. Since then, everything we know, and the vastness we have yet to comprehend, has been present as our Universe — or so Einstein's model and the Universe's expansion seem to indicate.

Powerful computer simulations suggest that soon after the Big Bang, the emerging Universe began to cool. This allowed the Big Bang's universal soup (think hyper-hot, sub-atomic, pure energy) to eventually condense to form hydrogen and helium atoms. Shock waves from the Big Bang resulted in slight gravity variations which, over time, gradually gathered these primordial atoms into cosmic gas clouds. Gravity naturally increased with mass, so as the gas clouds accumulated, their gravity became stronger and stronger. Eventually, that escalating process condensed gas clouds into stars, and gathered stars into galaxies that, even now are evolving. On occasion, galaxies even collide with each other. The Universe is continuously recycling and rearranging itself.

Stars are remarkably long-lived, but like everything else in physical creation, they are not permanent. Their mass is converted into energy via thermonuclear fusion. Some of that resulting energy is lost to the star as it is radiated out into the Cosmos. A familiar example is the radiation received on Earth, some of it as visible light, from our own resident star. Depending on its mass, rate of energy loss, and other factors, a star's fate can vary widely. It could explode as a supernova, expand into a red giant, or condense into a dwarf star, a neutron star, or a black hole.[xxix] Via nuclear fusion, stars are creating all the elements of the periodic chart. Supernovas then seed the Universe by dispersing across the Cosmos clouds of particles and chunks of matter eons in the making. Other stars' gravity eventually gathers this star material into solar systems with planets where life sometimes begins and evolves. All of this creative activity is still going on. The possibilities seem as endless as the Universe.

The law of nature that energy cannot be created or destroyed makes sense; that would be equivalent to God being created or destroyed. But energy has proven to be masterful at changing form. That is exactly the same thing as God expressing itself as creation. Creation never was a done deal that happened "In the beginning." It is an ongoing process *from* the beginning, that appears to have no end. The energy that is our Universe has been dancing around, rearranging itself, since its beginning. Of course, that applies to life here on Earth as well; nature is eternally evolving and shifting its expressions. But if creation has no end and is destined to remain eternally restless, does it make sense for it to have a beginning? This feels like another question beyond human capacity.

On a micro scale, the atoms and molecules that comprise your body are always coming and going. It is estimated that at this moment your body contains *none* of the same cells it did seven years ago; all of the several trillion of them have been replaced by new ones. It is absolutely true that nothing in physical creation is permanent. I sometimes wonder why we ever grow old since our bodies are always renewing themselves. But not understanding why my body is aging hasn't prevented it from happening.

As if the vastness of the physical Universe and the micro worlds within it weren't enough mystery, all manner of intangible energies like ideas, beliefs, dreams, fears, love, words spoken, thoughts entertained, memories, intentions, grudges, resolutions, emotions, and on and on, are also part of the Universe's total energy. All the invisible realms of heaven; angels, archangels, and unnumbered beings beyond human knowing, including the souls that animate every human being on Earth, are non-physical energies held within the Universe.

Physicists have recently estimated that the physical parts we can sense and measure could be thought of as the background noise of the Universe; only about *four percent* of its total energy.[xxx] For now, science has labeled the undetectable ninety-six percent as *dark matter* and *dark energy*. They are not physical, at least in the usual way, because they can't be directly detected or measured. Their presence was indirectly inferred, because the Universe contains far too little measurable (physical) mass to account for the gravitational bending of light as it passes around stars or other massive objects on its way from distant parts of the Universe to Earthbound telescopes.[xxxi] How an energy form can have the mass to exert gravitational force on light and still not be directly measurable is a mystery to this retired scientist. In any case, in some sense that awaits further understanding, it is literally true that *almost everything* is non-physical. It is true in parallel that there is far more to a human being than the physical aspects we can see and touch.

Quantum physics arose as a new branch of science because very tiny bundles of matter don't behave the same way big pieces do. Einstein's General Theory of Relativity breaks down when considering the subatomic realms. It's interesting that the mathematics associated with quantum physics do *not* require a beginning point in time for creation. Perhaps the Universe has always been, with no dramatic event to mark its beginning. Big Bang or not? — this is another question that, so far, lies beyond human discovery. My guess is that this may turn out to be another "yes, and..." example.

Steven Hawking has noted that so far in its long history, science has been concerned almost exclusively with characterizing *what* the Universe is, and has yet to address the question of *why* it exists at all.[xxxii] Although science has yet to prove or disprove the existence of causative factors, avatars and mystics have long believed that creation is the work of the God(s). As noted above, I believe God is one infinite energy field accompanied by the volition and intelligence that enables the creative process. God is both context for and content of creation. Creation can be seen as God revealing its infinite self.

My thoughts about the Universe and its origin story have spawned even more potential mystery about how it is behaving, at least in my mind. Scientific measurements indicate that the Universe's rate of expansion has been *accelerating* ever since the Big Bang — it's expanding faster and faster. In all our human experience, the expansive energy from an explosion dissipates with time. The initial expansion rate decreases with time until the energy settles into a dynamic equilibrium or static state. In my personal experience, I can't think of an exception. If eventual dissipation is how an explosive energy release behaves, and the Universe began with the Big Bang, then how can the Universe have been expanding at an *ever-increasing rate* for billions of years?! A few other questions were spawned by this question:

- What if the Big Bang was not a one-time instantaneous event? What if the *processes* of creation are also ever-evolving? Could it be that the Big Bang announced the beginning of a continuous release of creative volition, energy, and intelligence from the non-physical realms into the physical that has, so far, lasted for 13.8 billion years? And what if it has been happening everywhere, not just from a single point of origin? Would such a hypothesis better align with the Universe's actual behavior? Would it offer a bridge between classical and quantum physics?

- Such a hypothesis might suggest that the *energy and intelligence* behind creation is also expanding via on-going evolution. I have no idea how to explore the measurements or mathematics of such ideas, but it sure would be fun if some brilliant astrophysicists decided to explore them!

Love and wisdom:

I suggest we relax and accept that mystery will always be with us. Despite all the efforts of science and religion, human beings will never grasp the infinity of The Great Mystery. My heart knows and takes comfort in my deep belief that I live, and breathe, and have my being within, and am an integral part of, the energy field I call God. I am not separate from it in any way. The same is true for all creation. For me, that is sufficient.

A Mystical Morning

One early morning while on vacation along the northern California coast, I found a quiet corner in our small cabin and relaxed into my daily meditation. I noticed a pair of turkey vultures resting on the same branch in the pine tree outside our window that they chose for shelter the prior evening. They seemed to feel as secure as we did in our secluded vacation retreat. Out of the peacefulness a summary arose describing the flow of life in my seventh decade:

- *(Everything is) Holy Now*, a Peter Mayer song, has become a beautiful summary of my life.

- I have come to see family in each thing my awareness touches. Everything, from a blade of grass to the Cosmos, including the person in your mirror, is sacred. Seeing the sacred within myself opened the door to seeing it in all creation. I can now welcome and bless everything I encounter.

- I see life as a flow of experiences unfolding as all creation; we are participants. It is not a hierarchical system. Everything flows forth from within God, a holy energy that loves all expressions of itself equally, with no judgments or partiality.

- Each individual expression of life is God experiencing itself. You are that portion of the divine energy field having its life experience as you. Everything, from a subatomic particle to multiple universes shares this truth.

- "God is a circle whose center is everywhere, with a circumference that is nowhere." This wisdom is thought to have been first shared by the ancient Greek philosopher Empedocles, and later attributed to St. Augustine, Voltaire, and others. That wisdom is perfectly mirrored by creation. Quantum physics would say creation behaves like a hologram; the information of the entire Universe is present at each point within it. Thus, I am a center of the Universe; so are you.

- Evolution is the term Charles Darwin gave to the process by which physical life changes over time in response to changes in its environment. It is more than a physical process. Souls and all the beings in the heavenly realms also evolve toward ever more beautiful and loving expressions of God. Creation is an ongoing process. Because all that exists is God expressing itself, it follows that evolution is simply God expanding into its own potential. Maybe someday we'll figure out how an already infinite God could expand beyond what it already is.

Love and wisdom:

It is humbling to note that no matter where I look, love is present; it is always accompanied by endless mystery.

The Vision

"Your visions will become clear only when you can look into your own heart. Who looks outside, dreams; who looks inside, awakes."
— Carl Jung, *Letters, Vol. 1*

Sometimes in meditation, one encounters a silence so vast it defies description or explanation. It is like bathing in soft twilight lit from within. It always carries an unshakeable feeling of being loved with no exceptions or expectations. Although it lies beyond the physical, silence is not empty. The roots of all creation are anchored here. When one communes with God in the context of silence, there is peace and calm regardless of what is swirling in our world. Over time, silence teaches us that planning and control are only tools intended for use in response to divine inspiration and guidance.

Before meditation one morning, I asked for a vision to share with friends that would help them feel the vast space within themselves and catch a glimpse of who they are. Then my mind eased into that twilight silence described above. I allowed any thoughts that arose to float through without giving them my attention. They gradually ebbed, leaving calm unfocused awareness — until far off in the distance a faint speck of light arose like a barely discernable star. As the space between us dwindled, the speck became a ball of clear shining light. Closer still, it was a sphere of many shimmering windows with a breathtaking variety of sizes, shapes, and colors. As it moved closer and closer, it seemed as infinite as God.

Finally, it was close enough to see that each window had a name on its surface. A narrow green shaft of window caught my eye; its name was *grass*. I peeked into it and was stunned to see a boundless variety of grasses in a field extending in all directions beyond my capacity to see or even imagine. That single small window revealed all the grasses found upon every planet in the entire Universe that is blessed by the life of grass.

Nearby there was a very tiny window named *sand*. Squeezing small enough to peek through it, I was astonished to see an entire universe. In a holographic universe, the essence of an entire universe *really does exist* in a grain of sand! This whole sphere was a symbol of God itself. *Everything* was contained within it. It was clear that each facet of creation is a valid window into the essence of God, at the same time it is a unique expression of the whole.

As I explored around the sphere, I discovered an enormous heart-shaped, rose-colored window; its name was *love*. As I slipped through it into swirling magenta and lavender mists, I was stunned by overwhelming love enveloping me, saturating every cell of my being. God absolutely loves each of us beyond any condition whatsoever. That unbounded love is the primary gift and blessing of God. How you see yourself is your choice, but one wonders how a single moment ever arose when any of us thought we did not deserve love from ourselves. Yet, because we are creatures of choice, people often choose self-judgment and condemnation rather than self-love.

Exploring further, I encountered a window that was my own face. Just as a blade of grass or a grain of sand is a valid window into God; so are each of us. One's personal window is sometimes hard to see through. The view can be clouded by one's self-image, expectations, and judgments. Yet anyone who gazes upon your face is looking at a valid and beautiful view of God itself. Your view into yourself, or anyone looking into your window, is always clouded by the viewer's perceived limitations or biases. Each of us can see only what we allow ourselves to see.

Love and wisdom:

There are several points to highlight:

- What others' see is their business. Who you *are* is your concern.

- Now is the moment to embrace the choice to love yourself. It is the foundation upon which rests one's capacity to love everything else. The freedom and beauty of self-love will be obvious once you allow it.

- The huge-sounding attributes of God like omnipotent, omniscient, and omnipresent, are no more holy than the tiny facets of God like you, me, an endangered Preble's jumping mouse, a dandelion, or a microbe in your gut. Everything is sacred.

- A summary of ancient Egyptian teachings say we cannot understand or know God; we can only *be* God.[xxxiii] It is a clear invitation for us to stop fussing in our heads trying to understand life and move our relationship with God into our hearts. Our relationship with God calls us to *be* love.

- *Love* is the perfect summary name for the essence of God.

The Dream

"And when you want something, all the universe
conspires in helping you to achieve it."
— Paulo Coelho, *The Alchemist*

I had a dream during our second night at the Radha Madhav Dham Ashram in Austin, TX. That evening a video talk by the recently deceased founding guru had deeply resonated with me. He had emphasized that love is the center of all life and we can experience that love as our life when we get out of the way and allow it to naturally flow into and through us. Any apparent differences between his understanding and mine arose because of different cultural contexts and our choice of words to describe love. Such differences are only illusion when viewed through the eyes of God. The guru and I share a common understanding of love and life.

That night in a dream, I was out of breath and struggling to make my way through a rolling wilderness with broken forests and grassy hillsides; it reminded me of Crow Country in Montana. It was a windy, bitter winter night with an ominous darkness that only made it worse. I was fleeing from a single spot of light relentlessly pursuing me in the distance. Driven to exhaustion, I eventually fell into a snowbank unable to continue, awaiting my fate as the light approached. The now softened light shined forth from the face of a powerful, untamed woman, a dream-altered caricature of my daughter. She had been pursuing me to insist that I eat two crumbling fragments of sacred food. They looked like pieces of tamale, one made with meat and the other with vegetables. They were symbols of forgiveness granted and atonement accepted.

In the dream, I understood that the burden of life errors and resulting pain (karma) carried into this life from many prior lifetimes had been transformed by love and transcended during this life as Foster. The sacred offering was carried by my daughter because some of that karma was held in common by our souls. When I accepted and ate them, we were suddenly surrounded by a host of our ancestor spirits appearing as American Indians. I strongly felt their silent approval and the blessings they had come to convey. Their leader was the guru from the video at the Hindu Temple, only now he too was a North American Indian.

In only a moment they all faded and I awoke pondering the message the dream had brought. Details faded rapidly, so I tried to remember the feelings that accompanied the dream. It was clear that something profound had happened. It is hard for us to understand and grasp the power and blessing of finally transcending karma accumulated over many lifetimes. Joy rippled across the Cosmos touching many lives, some that seemed long ago from this realm of linear perceptions. The elation generated by transcending such karma is a joy unbounded by time and space.

The key message of the dream is the enormous blessings of this life as Foster, which reach far beyond the boundaries of this one lifetime. Each of us carries inherent within us opportunities beyond our knowing, until we embrace life's possibilities and allow love to carry us toward our destiny. This dream taught me that none of our lives is wasted and it is never too late for an experience of great meaning to emerge through us. When accumulated karma is finally transcended, blessings ripple across vast stretches of time and space impacting all the countless souls involved over many incarnations. Our karma is not confined to relationships with human beings. Our interactions with other aspects of creation also carry karmic energy. Each piece of creation is eternally connected with all the rest of it. It can take a long time to realize that all creation is our family, but that is our truth. The capacity to know the Cosmos as home is innate in all of us.

CHAPTER 5
THE NATURE OF HUMAN BEINGS

"In each of us, two natures are at war — the good and
the evil. All our lives the fight goes on between them, and
one of them must conquer. But in our own hands lies the
power to choose — what we most want to be, we are."
— Robert Louis Stevenson, *Dr. Jekyll and Mr. Hyde*

The reality of human beings is far beyond our wildest imagination. It is impossible, while anchored in human life, to grasp the vast nature of one's eternal soul. Yet, your invisible soul is as much a part of you as the Homo sapiens body everyone can see. The inner yearnings that pull you toward your higher potential are the voice of your soul. The part of you that questions whether you even *have* upside potential is the grumble of your Homo sapiens brain. In over-simplified terms, your soul is anchored in love, while the Homo sapiens nature is anchored in fear.

The marriage of body and soul thus unites two very complex and different natures in one human being. It is perfectly natural that we struggle with these two facets of our makeup! The dark and light flip back and forth, depending on which inner voice has our attention at any moment. Earthly life can feel like a roller coaster careening through a forest with sunlight and shadows flickering across our vision. But there is good news — as Stevenson says, we humans have "the power to choose," and we can choose to place our attention on the light.

Homo Sapiens — Children of Mother Earth

"Our closest living relatives include chimpanzees, gorillas, and orangutans. The chimpanzees are the closest. Just six million years ago, a single female ape had two daughters. One became the ancestor of all chimpanzees, the other is our grandmother."
— Yuval Noah Harari, *A Brief History of Humankind*

Isn't it amazing that the descendants of two great ape sisters born six million years ago are as different as today's chimpanzees and Homo sapiens? Yet, in some ways, the two species remain very similar. In recent years, scientists have succeeded in sequencing both the chimpanzee and human genomes. Both are enormously complex with billions of components. A National Institute of Health report stated that when everything is taken into account the human and chimpanzee genomes are 96 percent identical. [xxxiv] Physical evolution is so sensitive to genome differences, that two very similar genomes can result in remarkably different species over six million years. Over that time, hominids developed much larger brains than chimpanzees and voice boxes that could allow complex verbal expression. As a result, humans gradually developed spoken language and complex thought. The most recent hominid species, Homo sapiens, arrived on the world stage very recently; around two-hundred-thousand years ago. Over the past ten-thousand years our species has changed very little, yet daily life has changed remarkably. Our big brains have certainly learned how to modify our living conditions!

It seems obvious that our basic character hasn't kept pace with our explosive gains in knowledge. Imagine being born into a family clan of early humans wandering the savannahs of East Africa in an ongoing search for food, water, and shelter. Wild nature was also home to many other creatures doing the same thing, many of them larger and more powerful than our ancestors. So for early humans, staying alive depended on their ability to plan, communicate, and cooperate; accompanied by a finely-tuned ability to sense and avoid danger. Our ancestors were always alert, suspicious, fearful, and easily provoked to fight or flight. Hominids that failed to meet those criteria became some other creature's dinner. We are descended from the survivors and our basic nature still retains those *animal* instincts. Even now, we are superbly equipped to discern even minor differences in our surroundings, including other people. We are still naturally wary of unfamiliar situations and people that are not part of our inner circle of family and friends.

That same history also taught Homo sapiens loyalty and willing cooperation within their family groups — within that context we have always been loyal to each other and worked together. All those characteristics that assured our survival as a species a hundred millennia ago are still part of human nature.

Apparently, loyalty and cooperation on one hand, and easily triggered fear and anger on the other, create powerful opportunities for soul evolution. That complex Homo sapiens nature is what draws souls by the billions to incarnate here on Planet Earth. For most of us, life has made it clear that souls don't choose Earth because life here is easy!

The Nature of Souls is Rooted in God

"Your soul knows the geography of your destiny. Your soul alone has the map of your future; therefore you can trust this indirect, oblique side of yourself. If you do, it will take you where you need to go, but more important it will teach you a kindness of rhythm in your journey."
— John O'Donohue, *Anam Cara:*
A Book of Celtic Wisdom

I am deeply grateful to Michael Newton for knowledge and inspiration gleaned from his two ground-breaking books, *Journey of Souls* and *Destiny of Souls*. Newton was a psychiatrist and hypnotherapist who spent his pioneering career regressing thousands of clients into states of hypnosis *between* their earthly incarnations; this is distinctly different than *past life* regression. That allowed him to converse with the souls of his clients *in their spiritual home* through the voice and brain of their hypnotized bodies. Much of my belief system about souls is rooted in his work.

That does not mean I blindly accept Newton's work as a complete *gospel of truth* about souls. Obviously, all of his clients were souls who came to Planet Earth for experiential learning. That alone means his interviews covered only a tiny fraction of the consciousness found across the vast spectrum of souls that exist. His clients' descriptions of the heavenly realms are not perfect, nor are Newton's interpretations of their meaning. Both he and his clients were limited by their own finite consciousness. Throughout his lifework, souls and humans alike struggled with human language when trying to describe soul relationships and the beauty of soul life. In addition, no soul whose consciousness receives benefit from earthly incarnation is evolved enough to carry a complete understanding of Divinity and its realms. So, I see Newton's work as a breath-taking and beautiful picture of soul life, while at the same time it is only a partial picture. Despite my gratitude for Newton's work, the comments in this chapter represent my own beliefs, also limited by *my* consciousness and language skills.

Newton's work revealed that souls have many pathways to experience life and expand their consciousness. Incarnating as human beings on Planet Earth is only one of them. During conversations with two relatively advanced souls, Newton learned that souls are created by Divinity using a cloning process that throws off individual sparks of its own energy. The sparks emerge as unique immature souls that are incubated and nurtured until they are ready to join soul groups and begin preparation for their future. In fact, one of the two souls who revealed this had worked as an attendant in a neo-natal soul nursery. The key point is that each soul is a child of God from the moment of its creation. That heritage became part of us in our birth mother's womb before we were born.

My Homo sapiens personality is, sad to say, naturally over-sensitive, often fearful, and prone to anger. At the same time, the soul part of me is loving, wise, and generous-hearted. The arrangement by which my Homo sapiens body is hosting my soul during this lifetime has made for a remarkably interesting life. My soul is the innermost self I have come to rely on as my trusted friend and advisor. It is the heart of the person I am. I experience it as the presence of God within me expressing itself as my life. There is a similar divine essence at the core of every human being on Earth. Yet, our Homo sapiens personality often resists and resents this soul presence at the core of its being. This tension is an aspect of earthly life that makes human incarnation so powerful for soul evolution. It has taken most of my life to grasp this understanding of reality.

For those who wish to better understand soul life and character, I highly recommend Dr. Newton's books. I suggest they be approached with a curious mind and open heart: so much new information may be an uncomfortable contrast with long-held beliefs. Soul evolution is a process, so it is your choice to decide what you are ready to accept.

The Great Marriage

"Self-realization is the knowing in all parts of the body, mind, and soul that you are now in possession of the kingdom of God; that you do not have to pray that it come to you; that God's omnipresence is your omnipresence; and that all you need to do is improve your knowing."
— Paramahansa Yogananda, *Autobiography of a Yogi*

The marriage of Homo sapiens body with eternal soul has been the overarching common ground of humanity for a long time. The goal of souls incarnating as human beings on Planet Earth has always been their own evolution toward being love. Applied kinesiology has confirmed for me that over the past sixty-thousand years every human on Earth has hosted an incarnating soul for its entire lifetime. We are here to become beautiful souls.

Becoming a beautiful soul is not easy work; it could take thousands of lifetimes across dozens of millennia to embody that level of grace. But the spiritual growth that accompanies such effort, faithfully engaged for lifetime after lifetime, is exactly why souls choose to incarnate on Planet Earth. In fact, soul evolution is the primary purpose of human life. But what are souls evolving toward? Their north star is love; that is their direction. *Being* love is every soul's goal. Moving toward that goal is the aim of every human being, whether or not they realize it.

I don't know how many incarnations it took my soul to finally experience itself actually *being* love, a state I have realized in the latter stages of this life — some of the time. I have come to understand that love is who I am, and compassion is how that state of being is naturally expressed. If you want to get a feel for your soul's progress along this path, observe your life for evidence of compassion.

If you wonder what compassion looks like, think of Mother Theresa. Every day for decades, she lived her compassion for the most impoverished street people in Calcutta, one of the world's poorest cities. By her latter years she was a tiny wizened woman with minimal physical beauty in the eyes of the world. Yet, her energetic lifetime of compassionate action, made her beautiful heart and soul obvious to everyone.

Although my soul is far from Mother Theresa's depth and consistency of compassion, the following stories share experiences of soul evolution from my personal life. Perhaps they will inspire recognition of your own soul evolution.

There is Always More Than We Can See

Reincarnation had seemed like a reasonable concept to me for a couple of decades, but I hadn't realized how central it is to soul evolution until studying Michael Newton's *Journey of Souls*. Earthly life is very challenging, especially for relatively inexperienced souls; they are so used to life in their soul home where pain, struggle, fear, and suffering are absent. The innate fears, intense emotions, and contentious nature of the Homo sapiens brain provide a soul with challenges and meaningful experiences available in no other way. Souls understand that the great challenges of human life are accompanied by great opportunities.

On Earth, we are born as beings who need parental care for years while life matures us sufficiently to venture into the world more and more independently. Ideally, by the second half of life, we embody the spiritual maturity to consciously engage our life journey with intent and purpose. A human lifetime is a microcosm of the long arc of a soul's life. Souls have a similar pattern of gradual evolution carried out over a span of time that seems incomprehensible within the framework of a single human life. The soul Lahokam, hosted by my body during this lifetime, first incarnated on Earth nearly seventy-five thousand years ago.[xxxv]

Earlier I noted that souls are *born* via a cloning process from the very essence of God Itself. They are created with the purpose and destiny to expand in God-realization to the point where they again become inseparable from their source. Their own evolution is the process by which they approach ever closer to reuniting with the loving oneness that birthed them. Souls are thus born with a powerful instinct to evolve. Once a soul realizes that evolution is their sacred purpose, they become highly motivated to grow back toward their source. We could think of it as our cosmic homing instinct. In truth, all creation is an ever-evolving expansion that ultimately results in the expansion of God itself. That the already infinite God can expand is a mystery beyond human capacity to grasp, but my soul knows this to be true. Applied kinesiology confirms it.

Life experience has helped me better understand what it means to say life is a spiritual journey. Over the decades, life has gifted me with ever-emerging clarity about who I am and why I am here. Without my planning or control, key turning points arrived when saying "yes" carried events and meaning far beyond what I could see. Typically, speaking my yes allowed life to flow further along my soul's intended pathway than was anticipated. A key example follows:

Although I would not move to Colorado until my mid-thirties, I could feel the Rocky Mountains calling me west as a teenager reading my beloved outdoor magazines. It felt the same as the hills calling me into nature as a young child. When I completed graduate school in 1968, I actually received a job offer from the Department of Energy's plutonium processing plant at Rocky Flats, Colorado. My heart could feel the vast forests, rivers, and sky-scratching spires crying for me to come, but even in my youth I knew making nuclear weapons would absolutely shred my soul. I just couldn't do it; Colorado would have to wait.

So, the first stop in my career was with a glass container company in western Pennsylvania. My meticulous decision-making matrix had it ranked last of the four offers I was considering. But the first three choices each contained a *deal-breaker* that eliminated them. My left-brain analytical model was based on tangible information, while the deal-breakers were intuitive right-brain issues. The deal-breakers were my soul somehow making itself heard in ways I couldn't quantify. That first job provided an array of experiences in glass science and its practical application that supported my entire career. Looking back, it is very clear how that first career choice was in harmony with my soul's intended life direction. There were also layers of meaning within that choice that were completely hidden when it was made.

During the decade in Pennsylvania, I subscribed to *Colorado and the Rocky Mountain West*, a bi-monthly magazine that existed only a few years. It is now a bit of a classic; old copies from the 1970s are still for sale on the internet. Each issue featured a center section with eight scenic Rocky Mountain photos. After a few months, I often recognized the mountains before reading the captions. My emotional attraction to Colorado's mountains was also fueled by John Denver's songs about his love for Colorado. His music often brought tears of longing. By my mid-thirties, I had yearned to be there for twenty years, but all my efforts to open that Colorado door had come up empty. I finally gave up.

My wife and I purchased an old Pennsylvania farmstead and planned to build our dream home on its seventy-eight acres. The plans were drawn, the site was chosen, and the foundation dug. Only then, when I had finally surrendered my dream, did the phone call come. My decade in Pennsylvania was validated by knowing that the call would never have happened without the technical foundation in glass technology it provided. The timing was perfect. Had the call come a month later, too much investment in our new house would have made a "yes" response much harder.

The reason a decade of striving for my dream made no difference is simple. For many reasons, different timing would have resulted in missing enormous opportunities. The delayed unfolding of my dream is a lesson that life can be trusted. The move to Colorado unfolded with minimal effort; all I had to do was say "yes." It has turned out that finally living in my beloved mountains and a really fine job were only the first wave of blessings in Colorado. Other aspects hidden within that choice completely changed my life; a painful divorce, meeting my soulmate, and wave upon wave of spiritual growth. Life brought blessing after blessing with perfect timing, events I would have missed entirely if the move had happened sooner. Moving to Colorado even led to knowing myself as a being of love — who knew?!

Love and wisdom:

I am deeply grateful to be a published author in my second decade of retirement. Both Creation Is a Love Song *and my first book,* The Great University of Life, *are gifts to the world. They were born because I said yes to life in Colorado at the perfect time. I now bear witness that an enduring soul-calling, like my love of nature and Colorado's mountains, is not intended to remain only a dream. It is meant to be lived! Please, dear friends, honor your dreams and hold them with tenacity, trust, and patience. They are meant to be as real as my life now is. Do you have a dream awaiting your yes?*

The Cup

"Love conquereth all things."
— Mary Strong, ed., *Letters of the Scattered Brotherhood*

After meditating on this quote, I noticed a gift from my friend Paul, a potter from Iowa. It rests on the altar in my meditation space. The beautiful wine cup has a cream-colored base and pedestal, with the cup itself a rich reddish-brown. It feels authentic and substantial in one's hands, a reflection of the artist who made it. Gratitude flowed as I held it up as a symbol of the cup that I am. I was inspired to pray for unconditional love to fill me, that I might share it with the world.

While holding the cup, new clarity about prayer was received. If one is closed within, bound by a sense of separation from God, cup-filling is a struggle — an act of beseeching a far-off figure to grant a request. When one simply *is* a cup being filled, the love that best expresses their intent to serve the world naturally fills them.

Because the Beloved One already knows our every need, no words are needed to enhance the flow of love, wisdom, and peace. Open-hearted silent meditation is often more effective than words for opening our hearts to receive. Divinity is infinitely wise and generous, so everything we need flows into the cup that we are. But we are responsible for a critical step. We must believe in (trust) the cup-filling process. That trust *is* our readiness to receive, so our cup will always be filled *only* in proportion to our trust. When we are a cup held up to be filled, blessings flow to us most freely when our minds are quiet and we listen with our hearts.

The cup that you are can be tipped to pour the blessings you receive lavishly over the world. But only you may tilt the cup. If you tilt it only a little, the cup will remain full, but you will bless the world with less than your potential. Divinity will not overflow your cup to bless the world — tipping the cup is your job. To tip, or not, is part of the freedom of choice humans have been given. Because the Infinite Beloved is the cup filler, you can hold your cup upside down with no worry that it will become empty. The more you give in blessing, the more your cup receives.

One more key thing — there is no need to choose or control which blessings flow into and through you. Your pathway of service to the world is better guided by divine love than your intellect could ever manage. It has been wonderful to discover that everything you bless with love also blesses you at the same time. Blessings always flow in both directions. It is not a complex process; trust and willingness to *be* love are all it takes to move through life with grace. Why would we not be generous with all that we are?

Beauty is Everywhere

"If one truly loves nature, one finds beauty everywhere."
— Vincent Van Gogh, *The Essential Letters*

Our natural capacity to see beauty is often buried beneath the surface roar of daily life. In truth, beauty is always present in all physical and non-physical creation. After several years of wishing I could see creation as God sees it, that desire has gradually begun to open. There has been no specific process I could describe. Seeing beauty is more about having an open heart than what you are looking at.

Although I believe beauty is everywhere, for most of my life it has been rare for me to see it beyond the norm for our five senses. Heightened brightness of colors, crispness of objects, and clarity of air beyond my personal five-sense experience has happened only on a handful of occasions when the oneness of creation overcame the human illusion that I am separate from everything else. The effect seemed to happen of its own volition when I was sufficiently open to the presence of God. While those few occasions were transcendent, they typically lasted only from several minutes to a couple of hours. I have never been able to sustain it for long or *make it happen* by focus or mental effort.

Over the past few years, greater capacity to sense the beauty in nature has begun to open. It involves *feeling* the presence of beauty in addition to seeing it. When I relax into the presence of divine love, and recognize that it infuses everything, my gratitude seems to catalyze a deeper sense of beauty.

During a recent January, my wife and I were traveling through eastern Colorado to visit family in Kansas. Compared to the snow-covered mountains behind us, the rolling low hills were not visually inspiring; the ranchlands were a patchwork of mud, dormant grass, and dirty snow. Marilyn was driving, so I easily relaxed into a state of gratitude about many things. As I watched the flow of scenery, I began to feel love and joy vibrating just beneath the drab appearance of the land. In my mind's eye, the hills and barren trees were radiating curtains of magenta and purple light, tinged with green and gold. The colors were dancing like aurora borealis moving from the Earth upward. My entire being moved to a state of reverence. "My God," I thought, "It *really is* all holy." Gratitude for beauty changes everything as we move through life.

A Surprising Face of Love

"Love is an endless mystery, for it has nothing else to explain it."
— Rabindranath Tagore

A few years ago, I spent a weekend at the Franciscan Retreat Center in Colorado Springs. As their online brochure says, it "is a peaceful, breathtaking setting in the foothills of the Colorado Rockies in western Colorado Springs, but a world away from the city." I arrived on a Friday midafternoon with nerves a bit jangled after the hour-long drive in I-25's heavy traffic. After registration, I felt a need to calm and center myself, so I decided to locate and walk the labyrinth noted in their information packet. I found it in a grassy area next to an open forest behind and a bit away from the buildings. It was a comfortable day with shirt-sleeve weather, blue skies, and a gentle breeze. The scent of pines combined with the breeze to make the labyrinth especially inviting. As always seems to happen when I walk any labyrinth, life's stresses and daily distractions ebbed away as I gradually relaxed into a familiar sense of oneness and communion with God. By the time I reached the labyrinth center, a sense of deep well-being had replaced my jangled nerves and apprehensions about the weekend. My return trip through the labyrinth brought an increasing sense of gratitude and joy, an excellent way to begin my retreat.

Just as I reached the entrance portal, I felt a strong urge to do it all again. There was no-one else waiting to use the labyrinth and I had plenty of time, so I said a mental, "okay" and immediately began my second walk-through. The why behind this urge was quickly revealed as it became a remarkable time of communion with my mother, Vera. She had stepped over the threshold into her next life phase many years ago, but our soul friendship has continued to deepen since then. I can now see that the closeness of our mother/son identities had obscured our soul essences while we were both alive.

Walking slowly toward the center of the labyrinth, I was blessed to tell her I loved her as my mother. I knew she loved me deeply despite the pain her conservative religious views had brought to my childhood. Feelings of forgiveness accompanied words of love as the walk unfolded. But, the walk into the labyrinth was only the beginning of this experience. On my return from the center, for the first time in this life as her son, I actually *felt* and expressed deep love for her as my *daughter*. The power in the experience peaked when I actually spoke aloud, "I love you daughter Vera," over and over as I walked. During this second walk of the labyrinth, I actually experienced love for Vera as both mother *and daughter* from opposite ends of her earthly life. In that prior life, Laverne Hungerford loved her beyond words as an unexpected love child born ten years after her next older sister. In this lifetime, I once again experienced the wonder of that love during the labyrinth walk. Love that was deeply felt during my last lifetime as Laverne had somehow crossed the boundary into this life as Foster.

One outcome from this experience is deep gratitude for the power of multiple earthly incarnations as a vehicle for soul joy and growth. Now, I not only accept reincarnation as a concept, I have felt its majesty deep in my heart. I am grateful that the soul essence of mother/daughter Vera has felt it with me. The dance of creation blesses every one of us beyond our imagination as we move through life after earthy life. What an amazing gift!

"Sister"

*"Death could be looked upon as the birth canal into
eternal life. A little confining and scary, maybe,
yet it's the passage into a vastly fuller life."*
— Thomas Keating, *From the Mind to the Heart*

Beatrice Elaine Lunday and her two younger siblings were very close. Meghan and Drake had always called her "sister," as if it was her name. This story was written for them, and they have gifted me with their permission that it be shared.

I barely remember our first meeting with Beatrice. My wife and I had heard of "Sister" from her mother Edee and sister Meghan whom we had known for several years. But she didn't attend the church where my wife and I became acquainted with them. Then one late spring day Edee invited us to meet Beatrice at a local coffee shop. We talked for three hours, very impressed with her confidence and enthusiasm. She was in her early twenties and about to leave for Malawi where she would spend several weeks on a service trip. Her focus was also her passion; teaching the value of proper nutrition to poor women so their children could have a healthier start in life. She was motivated by the challenge of transposing her knowledge to fit the limited circumstances of life in a rural African village. We made a modest donation to help with her expenses and she was off to Africa. Upon her return, she returned to college in California, so we lost touch with her for the next couple of years.

Then suddenly, we became deep friends during a small group visit to Glastonbury, England that included both of us and several friends, among them Edee, Meghan, and Beatrice. The shift continued when our granddaughter Isabelle stayed with us for her first semester of college. Belle and Meghan became instant friends and Beatrice was around often. Bea had dropped out of college to face the mortal danger of inoperable brain cancer in the close embrace of her family. Chemotherapy bought time and hope that the medical community might be wrong; that somehow Beatrice's determination and enthusiasm would tip the balance in her favor. She returned to college and completed requirements for her master's degree, despite the tumor's return with renewed vigor. Beatrice revealed grace and strength that inspired all of us through her remaining months. Her family received her degree posthumously the spring after her death.

She must have had periods when the unfairness of life felt overwhelming. But if she allowed herself such moments, they were carefully hidden. Beatrice was so determined to milk the most from life, there was not much room for self-pity. She was a bundle of energy, even exploring her Scandinavian heritage in Iceland two weeks before her death.

Like most people, I had a set of beliefs about death before Beatrice. But living through her death with my *honorary grand-daughter* brought much deeper understanding. During her last few months, a group of friends gathered several times to meditate and pray for her. Only weeks before her transition, after several hours of prayer and meditation, I received a powerful message deep within, telling me that "this disease did not come to snuff out Beatrice's life, but to bring power and credibility to her work in the world." I was so convinced that I fully expected a miraculous recovery. Even as she lay in deep coma hours before her body finally gave up, I believed she would awaken with a near death story to inspire the world.

When the miracle didn't happen, my faith was shaken to its core. It felt like God had lied to me! For a couple of months, I was upset and angry because I had been directly told it was not time for her life to end — or so I thought. Then I was blessed to understand that Beatrice's soul, the wise and powerful architect behind her beautiful life, saw her death very differently.

After much thought, accompanied by release of my anger toward God, I woke up one morning with perfect clarity that it is impossible that my beloved God could mislead me. There had to be some deeper meaning connecting the message and Beatrice's death.

Then one morning, after weeks of wondering what it all meant, it was clear and obvious. I had simply misunderstood the message.

The context through which I viewed it was too small. I had thought it referred to Beatrice's *physical* life. I had longed to believe she would recover and not leave family, fiancé, and friends so early in life. Instead, the message had been anchored in the greatly expanded view of her soul's truth. As Michael Newton described in *Destiny of Souls*, souls do not die along with the body, nor are they, after death, surprised by a turn of events like a tumor in their body's brain.[xxxvi] When their body dies, no matter the circumstance, they simply return to their home in the realm of Spirit.[xxxvii] They contemplate the lessons from the life just completed, and make plans for their next incarnation. The soul's main purpose for incarnating is its own evolution and personal growth.

Beatrice's untimely death was heart-wrenching agony from our human point of view. But to her soul it was an experience of transcendent power and grace. The message I received is absolutely true, the lessons Beatrice lived and died to experience will indeed lend great power to her soul's work over many incarnations to come. Indeed, the malignant tumor's purpose was not to snuff out her life. Hers was a transcendent life, victorious and powerful beyond our human understanding.

I am deeply privileged to have known Beatrice even briefly. I am at peace that all unfolded with perfection, in spite of the pain that obscured that for some while. I believe our connection, so curiously close over her final months, was a gift exchanged between our souls. On one level, our friendship was new, yet we shared *instant* deep trust and love because, on a higher plane, we are soul friends. Knowing Beatrice helped me see life as a flow of experiences to support soul evolution, and death as rebirth from human limitations into the soul's natural unbounded state.

Beatrice Elaine, you were a gifted teacher. Your choice to persist with earthly life until Valentine's Day was perfect; my heart feels a surge of love and joy whenever you come to mind. Thank you.

CHAPTER 6

GROWTH, RESPONSIBILITIES, AND COOPERATION

"With nature's help, humankind can set into creation all that is necessary and life-sustaining."
— Hildegard of Bingen

We humans are involved in a multitude of roles over our lifetime. They naturally become more responsible and complex as our capacities grow through the decades from newborn to old age. Our experiences teach us about life by presenting a myriad of choices. Every one of them comes with consequences. The whole array of choices we make, our motivation when making them, and our response to their consequences, are primary tools for learning how to navigate earthly life and to grow into our potential. That's how soul evolution works.

As we approach adulthood, there are so many opportunities that planning our future can feel overwhelming. Similar moments can accompany any of the major forks in the road of life; marriage, divorce, career changes, retirement, etc. Often, the choices we make are driven by ego-based needs to feel secure, accepted, important, effective, successful, and so forth.

When making important choices, remember that your soul knows why it came into this life, and what direction is in harmony with your pathway. Souls communicate best through feelings, so listen to your intuition and trust your gut instincts. There is often plenty of advice offered by family and friends who want to help. Of course, you are free to consider all of it, but please have the confidence to trust your own feelings when you choose. *Do what you love* is good advice; it is often the best way to discern your soul's sense of direction. Listen to your heart.

Caretakers

Over the past twenty years it has become very clear that we have collectively fallen flat on our face as caretakers of Mother Earth. Science can identify the problems in detail, but it cannot change the basic nature of human beings that caused the mess in the first place. I believe our failures are telling us that, without divine guidance and inspiration, we cannot succeed as caretakers of each other, let alone Mother Earth. If one wishes to experience deeper connection with God, Mother Earth, and humanity, there are many approaches to a more inspired life. Some travel widely to be inspired by the world's beauty and varieties of life and culture.

Others may be deeply inspired without leaving their birth community. Exposing yourself to Mother Earth's variety of life and natural beauty can inspire your beliefs and whole understanding of life — but only if we allow those experiences to penetrate our hearts and minds. Exploration is more about having a curious mind and open heart than where you happen to be.

What exploring life looks like depends on how you define your playground. As a person with a current address, one's playground can be the property behind your house. As citizens of the Cosmos, the whole planet can be your playground. I have grown to know myself as a person with a fenced playground (my backyard) *and* a citizen of the Cosmos who attends school on Planet Earth. No matter how you define your playground, you have a responsibility as its caretaker.

Love and wisdom:

We chose to be on Planet Earth at this time to awaken and share ourselves with the rest of humanity. We are here to grow into responsible citizens of the Cosmos and caretakers of Mother Earth. None of us is here by accident.

Broken Promises

"The world, this palpable world, which we were wont
to treat with the boredom and disrespect with which we
habitually regard places of no sacred association for us,
is in truth a holy place, and we did not know it."
— Pierre Teilhard de Chardin, *The Divine Milieu*

Since the early days of Homo sapiens presence on Earth, our large brains and capacity for speech made room for the idea that we were superior to other species of life. In some ways we may seem to be better equipped than other creatures; in many ways, not so much. But, placing ourselves above the rest of creation has tainted our relationship with the natural world for untold generations. The advent of agriculture ten millennia ago signaled a new era of more intense manipulation of nature by humanity. During the last three centuries, the rapidly expanding industrial age greatly accelerated the imbalances humanity has brought to Mother Earth's web of life.

As a species, we grew up in a dangerous world where taking care of ourselves and our family was paramount — nothing wrong with that. But our species evolved with no clue that there was a caretaker role in our future. Caring for Mother Earth or other species was simply not on our agenda for most of human history; we were too busy taking care of ourselves. But things have changed. Our success has made Homo sapiens the dominant species on Earth. Our role as caretakers is desperately needed, but we are still waking up to the need for it. The status quo is hard to shift if one doesn't see the need for change. When a person finally comes to love Mother Earth as a holy place, being her caretaker is as natural as breathing. However, our millennia-old habit of using the planet to our advantage is so ingrained, it's sometimes hard to notice when our actions are out of harmony with that role.

Not all legally enforceable responsibilities are formal documents; e.g., before the advent of warranties, there was still an implied contract that a new wood stove would safely heat a home. This makes legal sense because both the supplier and the purchaser have rights enshrined in law.

The modern environmental movement has only begun to awaken to the fact that nature as a whole has inherent rights that need to be protected by law. To date, the possibility of a legal contract, implied or formal, between humans and nature exists in very few places. Ecuador has recently amended their constitution to provide legal rights for nature. Bolivia has passed legal protection for natural resources. New Zealand has enacted a law to protect a particular river with legal *personhood* (similar to granting personhood to corporations in the USA). A few local government jurisdictions around the world have taken similar action on behalf of nature. But most of the world has yet to embrace this embryonic aspect of the environmental movement. Because rampant pollution, degraded natural systems, and global warming threaten the entire web of life on planet Earth, the shift in mindset to legally protect nature is now necessary.

An example to reinforce the point: The Highline Canal was dug in 1879-1883 to supply South Platte River water to farmers and ranchers on Denver's dry plains. When local entrepreneurs persuaded English investors to support the project, they envisioned selling a million acres of land to thousands of ranchers and farmers. The canal's water rights, established in 1879, were preceded by many earlier-dated water rights, so the canal's claims were fairly *junior* in status. That meant that in dry years water for the canal could be limited. Perhaps investors from the rainy British Isles underestimated that issue.

It's hard to imagine in the twenty-first century, but local historical websites indicate the canal was *hand dug* from its origin in Waterton Canyon, southwest of Denver, to its end in present-day Aurora.[xxxviii] The canal meanders the land's contours, declining thirty-two inches for each of its seventy-one miles. Its hundred-foot right-of-way became a riparian corridor through the dry prairie soon after water began to flow.

An online dictionary defines an implied contract as "an agreement which is found to exist based on circumstances when to deny a contract would be unfair and/or result in unjust enrichment to one of the parties."[xxxix] Similarly, Wikipedia defines an implied-in-fact-contract as "a form of implied contract formed by non-verbal conduct rather than explicit words."[xl] These definitions, the latter in particular, suggest that the canal construction and operation represented an implied contract with nature. The big problem with this approach is that nature has never had legal status as an entity in most of the world, including the United States. Thus, nature has no legal status and the rule of law cannot apply. Historical records don't mention whether legal contracts existed between the canal owners and the ranchers and farmers supplied with water. But legal status, implied or not, was never recognized for the myriad plants and animals that came to live alongside, or in the canal when its water began to flow.

In the one-hundred-forty years since the canal was begun, the Denver area prairie has become the urban and suburban face of Colorado. The access road along the canal wanders through the ever-expanding metropolitan area and has become a long thin recreational park. Preserving the canal's "unique natural environment" was the number one concern voiced by people who participated in the Vision Plan meetings of the High Line Canal Conservancy. The Highline Canal Conservancy's Vision Statement is: "The High Line Canal's 71 meandering miles will be preserved and enhanced as a cherished greenway that connects people to nature and binds various communities together from the foothills to the plains."[xli] On March 8, 2017, The Denver Board of Water Commissioners approved a resolution supporting the Conservancy's Vision Plan. Their press release on that occasion recognized that the role of the canal has evolved over its life to provide more emphasis on recreation. That the canal provides riparian habitat for countless wildlife species along its entire length wasn't mentioned. Because nature has never had legal status, none of the parties involved recognized the implied contract with nature established in the mid-1880s when canal water began to flow.

In April 2016, conditions along the Highline Canal were much drier than I had seen in my thirty-eight years walking the canal path. Many of the huge cottonwood trees were dying or already dead. Great slabs of four-inch-thick bark had fallen under many of the decaying trees; some appeared to have been dead for several years. Fallen limbs were piled in windrows off to the side of the canal. Habitat for countless reptiles, mammals, insects, spiders, and more, for over a century, was disappearing before my eyes. There would be no new oriole nests like those swaying from earlier years. Nor would the cottonwoods any longer shade grasses and wildflowers along the canal's course. I have no idea how many cottonwoods have died along the canal's entire length; it could be thousands. It reminded me of the dead trees along meandering riverbeds gone dry in Arizona's deserts, where her sunbelt cities have taken water to support expanding populations.

High flows of spring run-off in 2015 had washed out the check-dam at the canal's origin, so there had been no water in the canal since early the prior summer. During my 2016 walk, the dying ecosystem felt like a broken promise. Today it seems like a sad case of a broken system. Too many people live along Colorado's Front Range to fit the available supply of water. The condition of the trees along the canal clearly indicates that the water had not been adequate to sustain them for several years prior to the check-dam failure. Dry winters with below average snowpack also played a role. The impact of rapid population growth along Colorado's Front Range seems like the real culprit. As is often the case, nature is the loser when humans want her resources. As painful as it feels, I am part of the problem.

One hopes that the seasonal flow of the High Line Canal can be restored so the ecosystem can regenerate. Nature knows how to recover, *if* the Denver Water Board is able to bring back the water. It would take decades for new cottonwoods to regrow, but in another century, adequate water flow could enable my descendants and their families to enjoy the shade of large trees graced with oriole nests along the High Line Canal. The Highline Canal is just one of uncounted thousands of similar *broken promises*, across Mother Earth.

Love and wisdom:

Lack of legal protection for Mother Earth does not release us from our shared role as her caretakers. All such examples point to a desperate need for healing our collective relationship with nature and all her creatures. To embrace our responsibility for all aspects of life is part of why we chose to be here in the twenty-first century.

Your Playground

Until two years ago, the playground behind our house for the prior thirteen years had been two and a half acres of open meadow and Gambel's oak thickets. Beauty often mesmerized me as the flowers and meadow of our yard flowed into the view from our deck across the broad West Plum Creek valley. Right below its railing were iris beds across its entire thirty-eight-foot width. They were classic dark blue irises with an intense scent that practically screamed *iris* at one's nose. While I enjoy some of the more recent hybrid colors, I do regret that the newly-attired irises somehow exchanged their classic aroma for a new wardrobe.

The view from our deck stretched from Long's Peak in Rocky Mountain National Park in the north, all the way to Pike's peak near Colorado Springs to the south. With its iris foreground, our view was especially gorgeous in springtime, when the various greens of meadow grasses danced in the breeze with light-green new Gamble's oak leaves and contrasting shades of dark juniper foliage. The patterns flowed and swirled across the West Plum Creek valley for several miles before blending into the foothills covered with deep pine-green forest. The foothills stood out against the snow-covered horizon of Colorado's Front Range with its pure blue sky. It sometimes looked like a long row of Bierstadt paintings standing side by side. To our west on summer evenings, clouds over Mt. Evans resulted in stunning sunsets with color intensities from subtle pastels to shocking bright and colors from peach to deep purple-reds and grays. Memory says no sunset ever duplicated another, yet, every sunset I invested with my attention, brought similar reverence and gratitude. I can't even guess how many thousand pictures my wife and I took. It's a good thing we had digital cameras by those years; film costs might have bankrupted us!

Our well permit wisely prohibited watering a lawn, so except for our flower beds, the land was in its natural state. An east-west gully south of the house was deep enough to be sheltered from the sun along its southern edge, so that part of the gully was a cool tangle of oak brush. Closer to the house, the sun resulted in a small grassy meadow next to the oak brush. That combination of shelter and food made the gully a favored place for mule deer to birth and rear their young. A particular doe raised twin fawns in the shelter of its oak brush for several years. In the third or fourth year, one of her daughters from an earlier year also gave birth in the gully, so there were three generations of deer; two moms and three fawns in our backyard. Especially when the fawns were little, the five deer got most of their water from our two bird baths and drained them once or twice daily. It was pure delight to occasionally witness the fawns' joyous enthusiasm as they raced and chased in and out through the brush and meadow areas.

An online search of coneflowers yields a bewildering array of names, shapes, and colors; ten species in all. It's not clear which of them were actually native to our historic prairies versus those created by cross-breeding efforts over the past century or so. Coneflowers once graced vast areas of North America's prairies and were valued by American Indians for medicinal purposes. Modern agriculture has drastically reduced their numbers, but when we first moved to our country house, a few yellow prairie coneflowers were growing in secluded corners behind our house, mostly in the margins between brush and meadow. Individual blooms would hardly draw one's attention; an exaggerated spiky brown cone with a small cluster of yellow bracts around the base to attract pollinators. The actual flowers were so tiny they were barely discernable, with a few hundred covering each inch-long central cone. I had never seen prairie coneflowers before in the wild, but had read about them at a prairie museum in Topeka, KS a number of years ago. I thought these might be quite rare in today's world, so I began collecting their seeds and scattering them over ever-expanding areas of our property year after year. I was glad the deer and other wild creatures weren't inclined to eat them. In larger stands, when blowing in the breeze, they are transformed into dancing fairies of bright yellow. We grew to appreciate their beauty all around our property after several years. The magic of this backyard playground made this my favorite of the dozen or more homes occupied over my nearly eight decades.

Love and Wisdom:

The natural beauty of animals and wildflowers can bring heaven on earth into our daily lives. What better reason to be responsible caretakers?

Whimsical Mystical Garden

The new responsibility of breadwinner arrived before my senior year of college. Our newlywed finances were not robust. My wife's neighbors offered to let us use some garden space, so we planted several rows of vegetables. The green beans flourished better than the others, so we ate them all summer and canned fifty-four pints.

After college I continued my gardening efforts, but career priorities left little time for it. After a few years, I stopped trying. The next thirty-five years brought half a lifetime worth of changes, but as for gardening, an occasional tomato plant was about it. When my second wife and I moved into our country home in 2005, it came with flower beds and pots, so we decided to have flower gardens. The neighborhood mule deer gratefully munched everything except marigolds, irises, and a bed of native wildflowers. For the first five or six years we planted no vegetables on our modest acreage.

Given that history, imagine my surprise when I awoke one late-autumn day a few years ago full of enthusiasm to create a vegetable garden. Early winter was warm enough to fence a triangle of land. Intuition led me to include a patch of oak brush, rather than clear it or fence it out. Layers of sandstone just beneath the surface meant raised-bed gardening, so seven of them were built and placed within the perimeter along with two horse troughs. Chicken wire on the posts would wait until the planters were filled with topsoil.

By mid-March the vision for the garden was becoming whimsical. Flowerpots were hung on either side of the gate, with wind chimes tinkling, and trinkets sparkling from the oak brush. Prayer flags and ribbons fluttered along wires between the tops of the fence posts. A bench was placed beside the oak brush so the whimsical gardener could commune with nature in the shade. I even placed a small stand next to it for my CD player; there would be music in the garden.

After the fencing was installed, wooden signs were created to make clear my intention for the garden. "Shakti's Garden" was hung over the gate, with "Earth Mother" and "Sophia" hung on two sides of the fence. "Joy!" and "Love" were staked in the two beds along the driveway. I also installed a soaker-hose system. I had high hopes the plants in this garden would be happier than the neglected veggies from my early gardening years.

The results were mixed that first year. A nasty hailstorm pushed the pause button on the whole garden for two weeks; the plants with robust root systems fared better. Overall, despite the hailstorm, the garden did reasonably well. More compost and mulch would have helped. So, I built a compost bin and asked in-town friends for lawn clippings. Next year would be even better.

There was a wonderful experience that first year in the garden. I was playing music for the plants, a CD from Damanhur,[10] a spiritual community in northern Italy. They had developed a technique where electrical signals from various plants were fed into a synthesizer. The resulting music was unique for each type of plant. I had just begun playing music created by anthurium, a genus that includes several flowering plant species, when a pair of mountain bluebirds came and sat on adjacent fence posts. They appeared to be mesmerized and sat there with me for twenty minutes. When the CD ended, they flew off to continue their day. I sat for several more minutes pondering the bluebirds perfect thank-you in silent gratitude. Quite an affirmation for creating the garden!

Love and wisdom:

When we work with Mother Nature to co-create beauty, she responds in kind. Expressing beauty is a key part of her character. We can choose to be part of that process.

---

10   http://www.damanhur.org/en/the-damanhur-shop

Learning to Cooperate with Nature

"Be brave. Take risks. Nothing can substitute experience."
— Paulo Coelho

Results from the garden's first year were encouraging, but its gardener was still in kindergarten. One motivation for our organic garden was healthier food. Another was the harmony I felt working *with* nature rather than trying to control the gardening process with chemical fertilizers, pesticides, and herbicides. It seemed ironic that working with nature felt more complicated. Each type of plant has its own specific needs; so ideally, nutrients, water, and sun exposure should be individually optimized. This tuning process requires knowing the unique characteristics of your plants, the garden's soil, location, and climate. By choosing to forego chemical agriculture, organic methods also ask the gardener to facilitate a natural balance of all life in the garden; plants, flowers, weeds, field mice, salamanders, toads, insects, spiders, and so forth.

If we each had to start at the beginning, and trial and error was our only way to learn, organic gardening would be overwhelming. But, since gardening has been essential to human life for several thousand years, relevant know-how has been passed down the generations as naturally as DNA for millennia. It is interesting to note that my sister and I, born in the 1940s, were the first generation of our family in centuries *not* to grow up on a family farm. But Dad did have a big garden behind our house.

Agriculture began *organic* and stayed that way until invention of industrial fertilizers in the early twentieth century. Increased productivity led to wide-spread use by mid-century. In the decades since then, chemical pesticides and herbicides have also grown into widespread use. The negative impacts from all these chemicals on Mother Earth's web of life are a litany of willful ignorance. We turned our back on negative consequences in our haste to increase productivity from the land. Today, much of America's cropland is owned or controlled by agribusiness corporations. Turning plant-raising into an industry and animals into production units has taken the heart out of modern food production. Migration away from family farms into cities and suburbs over the past century has caused many Americans to lose touch with their family heritage as gardeners and farmers. Many have also lost touch with nature itself. By choosing to create a garden, I found reclaiming lost knowledge to be a lot of work. But the close working relationship with nature brought much deeper meaning to gardening. It helped me see that nature is an important facet of Divinity.

It has been forty years since I first read *The Magic of Findhorn*.[xlii] Paul Hawken told the fascinating story of a new-age spiritual community in northern Scotland where magical events regularly occurred in their gardens. It stirred in me a nostalgic longing for such experiences, but it seemed to carry no more relevance for *real* life than a child's fairytale. The book sat there for decades gathering dust alongside other inaccessible dreams. A few years ago, when interest in organic gardening awakened, I did what any retired scientist would do; I read books about the science of organic gardening. *The Magic of Findhorn* was not on the list.

That would change in mid-2016 when a friend recommended a book, *Living as if the God in All Life Mattered*, by Machaelle Small Wright. That led me to her *Perelandra Garden Workbook*. Machelle is a down to earth, detail-oriented author a scientist could trust. She claimed *The Magic of Findhorn* had changed her life. She had spent three months at Findhorn and became a working colleague of Peter Caddy, one of the co-founders of Findhorn. Machaelle confirmed the Findhorn stories in her own garden, and provided detailed techniques for working with "devas" and "elementals," the nature energies that support the lives of plants and animals. The clincher for me was her use of applied kinesiology to communicate with them. I had used it for years to clarify and confirm my beliefs about many spiritual matters. How exciting it would be to relate directly with nature about the specifics steps to create my own magical garden!

The next two summers were transition years for the garden and the gardener. Using Machaelle's techniques, establishing connection with nature seemed straightforward. It took practice to effectively ask a series of yes/no questions that accurately reflected nature's thoughts, but I learned to gather information that was clear and useful. I followed nature's advice on what, where, how, and when to plant each item in the garden. The new garden would include both beauty and food. A variety of vegetables shared space with lots of flowers and herbs. Most of them grew well, but the gardener will always have more to learn.

The best example of nature's advice being successful was not in the fenced garden. Two years earlier I had reworked the flower beds on the south side of the house, planting a dozen rose bushes and several other perennial shrubs. Soil conditions were not robust and the new plants languished. They were surviving but growing slowly with no flowers. I did not have Machaelle's extensive array of natural soil amendments, so I asked nature to work with what was available. The deva for those beds said the plants' water levels and mulch were fine. The local garden store had composted cow manure and a mix of sheep manure with peat moss. I also had a mix of well-aged horse and alpaca manure from the same friend who had introduced me to Machaelle's books. The deva's recommendation was two small shovels of the horse — alpaca mixture for each plant. I was to pull back the mulch, place the manure, water moderately, and replace the mulch. It took a lot of questions to get that much detail. Two weeks later, all the plants were blooming!

Shortly after we moved to our rural location, packrats chewed through the wires connecting the alternator to the battery of my car. We discovered the mischief when the battery had barely sufficient power to reach our destination thirty miles from home. When I switched the car off, it was dead. So, my wife watched our grandson play hockey, while I arranged for a tow truck — not the best part of my day.

The irritation faded and I spent the next few summers working on wildfire mitigation by clearing and trimming the oak brush surrounding our house. Creating safe distance around buildings is important in the dry prairie — mountain transition zone near

Colorado's foothills. Rather than haul the brush away or run it through a chipper, I piled it on our property away from the house. I recall thinking it would provide nice wildlife habitat, not even thinking about the packrats. With my generous donation of new habitat, they had a major population explosion! They are nocturnal creatures, so we saw them only occasionally when sitting on our deck in the evenings. What we saw every morning was their overnight gift of rat poop on the front porch and deck of our home. We called in reinforcements, a local pest control company. Their strategy was to place poison bait stations around the perimeter of the house, including the deck. We were suddenly overrun by packrats, so delighted with their new food supplies that they even built a nest inside one of the bait stations! Their breeding proved fully capable of keeping pace with the death rate from the poison bait. The situation simply didn't get better, so after a year we bid the pest control company farewell. By then I was learning to communicate with nature about the garden, so I tried asking the packrat nature deva what to do. (Yes, there is a deva for packrats!) The response was instant, not even requiring yes / no questions. I heard the words in my mind, "Get rid of the brush piles." Just to be sure where it came from, I confirmed via applied kinesiology that it was indeed the deva. I spent the next two months dragging seven dumpster loads of brush from the far corners of our property. Dozens of rats were evicted by disassembling the rent-free condos I had created. I also scattered many bushels of acorns from their food caches. The poor rats responded with the desperation of the newly homeless, even invading geranium pots and building a nest beneath the gas fire pit on the deck.

Eventually, the eviction strategy seemed to work; by the next year, the rats had resettled over a wider area and the invasion had calmed. Nonetheless, every fragment of rat signs anywhere around our house triggered fear that they were staging a comeback. We had learned the valuable lesson that *cooperation with* nature worked better than trying to *manipulate* nature. But the rats left some deep emotional scars.

The following summer I reworked our flower beds to minimize potential rat habitat. I also did maintenance on the lower half of the house. I have never enjoyed being more than a few feet above the ground, so our two-story house reminded me how uncomfortable I am with ladders. It had gotten worse with age. Those two summers made it clear that property and house maintenance had shifted from enjoyable hobby to drudgery. My age was telling me it was time to move.

For six weeks I couldn't make myself say yes to the obvious. I knew we needed to go, but I hated to leave our spectacular view and the land. After seventy years of loving nature, I had never felt so closely connected. I was afraid that when we moved to town, my friendship with nature would shrink to fit a small suburban lot, or disappear altogether. If aging required me to let go of nature, I could see life drifting into to ever-darker shades of gray.

In September, we scheduled a visit with a realtor friend to discuss numbers so we could see how the finances of moving might work out. By the time she arrived a few days later, everything had shifted. She sat down with us on a Monday afternoon and I surprised everyone, including myself, by saying "It's time;

let's do this thing." The house was placed on the real estate multi-list Thursday morning. We had two showings and two offers, at and above the asking price, that same afternoon. We had a contract to sell our home by Friday afternoon. Now we had to find our next house. On Saturday we looked at five nice houses that met our criteria, but something seemed not quite right about each of them. Within fifteen seconds of entering the sixth one, we looked at each other and said in unison, "This is it." Our realtor joked that maybe we should look at it before deciding. We did and it confirmed our intuition. The house had come back on the market that very day, after an earlier sale fell through. The owners were eager to sell and had reduced their asking price so that it fit within our range. They accepted our offer. Within one eventful week we had agreed to sell our old house and purchase a new one. I have become accustomed to sensing support from the spiritual realms, but that series of events seems especially clear. Like many real estate transactions, there were complications, but in the end those several separate events were resolved with exquisite timing so the whole process fell into place like a fine-tuned watch. We remain truly grateful for the other-worldly flow that brought us into our new home.

The fear that leaving our country house would end my connection with nature proved to be unfounded. I learned that my connection with nature lies within me, not in some particular location, even though it flowered beautifully in that particular setting. The first months after moving, I missed our spectacular view and the animals, especially the deer and birds. But early that spring bluebirds, swallows, and house finches often visited our new small yard, so I felt much better.

In my self-imposed funk over leaving my nature haven, I chose to give away many of my garden and yard tools, planning to hire all the yardwork and have no garden at our new home. I really thought I was done with that phase of life. But the longer and warmer days of spring reawakened my desire to do some yard projects and buy new flowerpots. Our yard will again be a flower and songbird haven. The nature spirits and I are eager to plant.

Love and wisdom:

When life seems to be shrinking or moving away from us, it is a sure sign that an opportunity to learn and grow has begun. Happiness and joy naturally flow when we say "yes" and lean into that opportunity.

The Big Playground

"To me, it seems a dreadful indignity to have a soul controlled by geography."
— George Santayana, *The Life of Reason*

"...a man's mind is stretched by a new idea or sensation, and never shrinks back to its former dimensions."
— Oliver Wendell Holmes, *The Autocrat of the Breakfast Table*

By the mid-1990s, I had traveled overseas occasionally for two decades to meet with other technical people. The purposes and agendas of those trips remained comfortably in my glass technology comfort zone. The countries visited were all first world economies and my hosts spoke fluent English. So, those experiences provided minimal exposure to the unique cultural aspects of the host countries. My interest in the world's variety of people, cultures, and history had yet to be kindled.

That naivety was taken away by Mexico and Honduras in the mid-1990s. I had joined the Board of Directors at a Denver non-profit whose focus was serving their Latino community. Several times, my wife and I accompanied some of the staff to various Mexican cities in the company of senior citizens from the community. The trips were focused on reconnecting the seniors with their cultural roots. They were low-budget affairs so we stayed in Mexican hotels, and traveled about the country via local buses.

It's hard to overstate the value gleaned from actually *feeling* life as it is lived in Mexico. It brought a new beginning to travel in cultures different than our own. Mexico piqued our interest, deepened our confidence, and expanded our comfort zone. We learned that Mexico's culture is as varied as the USA, with a vast richness of history, music, dance, and art. There were excellent museums and open-air markets everywhere with a bewildering abundance of history, food, consumer goods, and handcrafted items; even tools. It became very clear that the USA is just different, not superior, to everything beyond our borders. A few examples will show how Mexico opened our eyes and taught us how to be comfortable with exploring this beautiful planet.

After Columbus discovered the Americas, Mexico's interactions with early European invaders, particularly Spain's conquistadors, began a century earlier than the rest of North America. Coronado was utterly bedazzled in November, 1519, when he was first welcomed into Tenochtitlan, the Aztec Empire's capital, on an island in the middle of what was then Lake Xochimilco. In what is now the center of Mexico City, he found sophistication and beauty the equal of any city in Europe. It's challenging to imagine lives of such idyllic grandeur as the upper levels of Aztec society enjoyed in the early sixteenth century. We visited an archeological museum that preserves and highlights much of that era's history, located just off the zocalo (main square) in this city of thirty million people. We also visited the preserved remnants of Tenochtitlan's famous gardens which once graced the shores along the lake. A day experiencing the narrow canals between the raised gardens was a crowded, crazy, and fun rumba of colorful, hand-poled boats, today's tourist replica of the Aztec craft of yore. That experience let us glimpse another facet of what Coronado saw centuries ago. To bring some balance to this short review of the Aztec capital, their culture was not without its horrific side. Human sacrifices, especially of conquered enemies, was extensive enough that the streets sometimes literally ran red. Such a powerful contrast of extravagant beauty alongside exaggerated violence! Regardless of Coronado's motivations and first impressions, Spain's war technology, including metal weapons, and horses, coupled with her craving for Aztec silver and gemstones, soon led to devastating decline of Aztec power and opulence.

Perhaps the most remarkable architectural achievements of pre-colonial Mexico are on display at another nearby site. Twenty-five miles northeast of Mexico City, lies the site of another city that thrived for half a millennium beginning 1500 years prior to Coronado's central Mexico visit. From 0 to 500 CE, Teotihuacan, a city of at least 125,000 people, was the largest ever in the pre-Columbian Americas, and the sixth largest in the world in its era. Today it is famous for its gigantic temples, comparable in size to the great pyramids of Egypt. Most of the restoration to date encompasses the ancient city's center with pyramids, broad streets, and other ceremonial buildings. The pyramids were temples to honor the major gods of the culture that built them. The two largest honor the sun and moon gods. A walk along the very wide, mile-long main street, and a climb of several hundred feet up their steep sides to stand atop the main temples gave us a glimmer of what was required to build these immense construction projects. They were begun nearly two thousand years ago, by a people with no draft animals or modern tools. They also carry echoes of a culture with administrative skills and other resources that could carry out such enormous projects. Mexico's pre-colonial history carries implications that command deep respect when held up alongside the relatively modest architectural and cultural development elsewhere in the world at the same time. To me, the accomplishments on display at Teotihuacan seem as impressive as the ancient Acropolis in Athens or pyramids and other tombs along Egypt's Nile River. Similar comments could be made about the Mayan or Aztec ruins.

Today's Mexican culture is a unique blend of Spanish and

pre-Columbian cultures, with a sprinkle of French influence in the 1860s when they briefly subjugated Mexico. The Mexicans sometimes brush aside this French intrusion with, "We threw the French out, but kept the bread." And it's true; the bread served in Mexico City was comparable with any we've eaten in Paris.

Our visits have included silver mining towns like Taxco and Guanajuato, high in their mountains, to beach resorts like Acapulco and Puerto Vallarta. One of the best anthropology museums in Mexico, of the many we've visited, was in Veracruz, on her southern Gulf coast. It featured the ancient Olmec people of that region, famous for their enormous sculptures of human heads. We have been to industrial cities like Monterey in her north and centers of strong indigenous influence like Oaxaca in her far south, along with several other places across Mexico. We've sampled a broad array of local cuisine, including a favorite mole sauce that originated in Puebla. We've attended a folk-dance review in a Mexico City museum, heard mariachi music in Guadalajara where it originated, collected pottery, stories, flavors, and impressions of amazing variety across Mexico. In my opinion, Mexico offers a cultural palette as rich as France, the United States, or any other nation on Earth.

I'll close this burst of enthusiasm for Mexico with an example of an interaction I had with ordinary Mexican people. All three times we visited Mexico City, we stayed at Hotel Catedral, a small, relatively inexpensive, Mexican hotel just around the corner from the zocalo behind the largest cathedral in Mexico. The church itself has a name as long as its monumental size. "The Metropolitan Cathedral of the Assumption of the Most Blessed Virgin Mary into Heaven" is the seat of the Catholic Archdiocese of Mexico. It sits atop the sacred Aztec ruins from an earlier era on former swamp land that is sadly inadequate to stably support its enormous weight. Its chandeliers thus hang at odd angles from the columns, and so forth, such that to an untrained eye, it looks dangerously unstable. The cathedral was begun in 1573, just fifty-four years after Coronado's first visit, thus illustrating the rapid collapse of Aztec culture under Spanish domination. The cathedral was built in three major stages over the next 280 years, so it's been standing in its present configuration for over two hundred years. So, despite its strange angles, with a lot of structural maintenance, the cathedral endures. Although, I wouldn't want to be inside during a major earthquake!

We ate breakfast at the Hotel Catedral each morning before our day's adventures and got to know some of the servers well enough to enjoy limited conversations. They were interested in improving their English, and several of our group were pretty competent with Spanish. One day a young server approached me with a question. He wanted to know the English word for the yellow center of an egg. None of our fluent Spanish speakers were seated at our table. The linguistic gyrations we went through before I understood what he was asking had him, and our table, laughing out loud. The answer, yolk, was anticlimactic compared to the fun we had figuring out the question.

Compassion was added to the blessings from international travel by service trips to Honduras, a small Central American nation nestled amongst Nicaragua, El Salvador, and Guatemala.

All Central American nations hold in common their cultural heritage from the Mayan people. Copan is the main ruin in Honduras and we visited it each time we went there. By our last visit, going to Copan felt like a pilgrimage.

Even more than two decades ago, Central America was a far poorer, significantly more dangerous, part of the world than Mexico. Our trips were hosted by a couple associated with the well-known charity organization, Heifer International. The husband from Indiana had the US connections to maintain the funding relationships that supported their work, while his Honduran wife with Mayan heritage possessed the powerful sense of purpose, drive, street smarts, and guts to orchestrate their daily lives and work. Together they were a formidable team; without Tim and Gloria Wheeler, we could never have put together the rich experiences of serving the world in Honduras. They have since retired to Indiana, and Central America is more violent and dangerous than ever.

During our four service trips, we were volunteer labor, working alongside local Hondurans on projects that belonged to them. One year, we helped enlarge a barrio church in Tegucigalpa, their capital city; another time we assisted with adding a room to the health clinic in the rural, very isolated village of La Rinconada. A favorite memory was visiting a small Mayan village in the hills outside La Esperanza, where Heifer International had provided a few chickens and goats. Some of the farmers were having a picnic near the village on a hilltop with an expansive view when I walked by. Using one of my few Spanish words, I waved at the view and said, "Buena vista (Beautiful View)." They smiled and nodded in agreement. For me, that small connection was the most meaningful part of our brief visit. Those visits to Honduras were our first experiences sharing the joy and sweat of working with and getting to know ordinary people whose lives were very different than ours. Now that our hearts were involved, we were hooked.

Marilyn and I are deeply grateful for our powerful experiences in Mexico and Honduras. They opened the floodgates, so that in the two decades since our retirement began, we have been blessed to visit more than twenty countries, on every continent except Australia and Antarctica. Alphabetically speaking, we have been from Anchorage to Zurich, and visited several countries multiple times. Some of our trips were spiritual pilgrimages that blew away the boundaries of our lives and worldview. Travel brought friends around the globe and we have become citizens of the world. It's almost impossible to overstate the positive impact of world travel on our lives.

I am not suggesting travel all over Planet Earth is necessary for spiritual growth, but it has supported ours. Beauty is everywhere and people are an important face of beauty. Déjà vu experienced when you *know* you have previously been in places never before visited in this lifetime, can open priceless revelations about life. Having friends beyond our country of origin makes the world feel friendly and more intimate. *Friends* can include places and animals too; even mountains can feel like one's children! But everyone gets to define *far from home* for themselves.

The environmental impacts of travel are not trivial. Releasing combustion products of jet fuel high in the atmosphere makes them especially damaging. On one hand, the greenhouse gases generated by travel are easy to quantify; the blessings of spiritual growth don't come with numbers. There are ways to lower environmental impacts of travel if one is motivated. I cannot second guess our travel experiences; they have profoundly shaped who we are. But so have experiences with nature in my own backyard and meditation inside our house. Here is some *food for thought*: I'd much rather *visit* Argentina, Chile, or New Zealand and give up eating fruits flown via jet from these same countries to our grocery store in the winter. "Think global and eat local" is a fine concept! Balancing environmental impacts and the blessings of travel are a personal set of choices.

Love and wisdom:

Once you commit to a life of spiritual growth, it is breath-taking to experience the Universe opening doors to bring that intention into reality!

CHAPTER 7
EMBRACING THE GORILLA

"Watching your daughter being collected by her date feels like handing over a million dollar Stradivarius to a gorilla."
— Jim Bishop

The first six chapters have highlighted the path that brought me into loving relationship with God and Mother Earth. Love has mostly replaced fear in my psyche, but my optimism is still guarded about the future of Mother Earth and humanity. We have collectively created enormous global problems that beg for our attention. This chapter is about being real as we approach the future. It is completely irresponsible to ignore global warming, or hope it will go away on its own. The above quote captures how I feel about turning Mother Earth over to global warming, but none of us can reverse it on our own. This chapter describes what we face and what is required of us.

Love and wisdom:

The crises of these times, including the coronavirus pandemic and global climate change, are a common ground for humanity; powerful signs that our time to shine has come. Indeed, we chose to be alive on Earth now. Every life form that shares Mother Earth with us awaits humanity's response. Despite the gravity of our circumstances, there is no lack of resources. We have everything we need! The only question is our collective commitment.

Global Warming

"To be clear, climate change is a true 800-pound gorilla in the room. The effects of global warming threaten global environmental upheaval over the coming century. But for South Florida and the Everglades, it could be the death knell if urgent action is not taken."
— Debbie Wasserman Schultz, U. S.
House of Representatives, Florida

"It is a predisposition of human nature to consider an unpleasant idea untrue, and then it is easy to find arguments against it."
— Sigmund Freud, *A General Introduction to Psychoanalysis*

If it were up to me, Rep. Schultz quote would sound even more urgent. Global warming is already disrupting the lives of humans and other life forms across the globe. We are on the leading edge of a mass extinction of species like the world hasn't seen in many millions of years. It is a slow-motion disaster of the first magnitude. The planet weather system is huge and moves so slowly that there is an illusion that we have plenty of time to fix it. It has enough inertia so, based on Freud's observation, there has been plenty of time for climate change denial to become entrenched around the globe. The truth is, we have no idea how much time is available to reverse the alarming trends. New information reveals that conditions may be even worse than we had thought. We are dangerously close to the turning point where the momentum of global warming can no longer be reversed.

Let me explain: Although our understanding of the greenhouse effect at the root of global warming has so far centered on carbon dioxide in Earth's atmosphere, we are just becoming aware that methane is a significant added threat. Methane released into the atmosphere persists for about twenty years on average, before being naturally converted to carbon dioxide and water. Carbon dioxide persists in the atmosphere for about one hundred years. The bad news is that while it exists, methane is about 26 times more potent than carbon dioxide as a greenhouse gas. So, even though the current level of atmospheric methane is about $1/200^{th}$ that of carbon dioxide, methane accounts for about twenty percent of global warming.[xliii]

Drawdown: The Most Comprehensive Plan Ever Proposed to Reverse Global Warming, edited by Paul Hawken, showed that technology which is already available, if implemented at feasible levels by 2050, would lower atmospheric greenhouse gases enough to reverse global warming.[xliv] Under that scenario, the key question would be whether humanity collectively chooses to respond *in time*. So far, the world's governments seem to be moving at a pace which will use all the time we have available. That is a risky approach considering we don't know how long that is!

Drawdown included the effects of methane from known sources, like food production and fossil fuel operations. Since it was published, steps taken to reduce those emissions should have resulted in lower atmospheric levels of methane by now, but instead, they have gone up. Unfortunately, the climate change models when *Drawdown* was published did not include methane from a new phenomenon discovered since its publication: methane bubbling in thermokarst lakes in the arctic regions of Siberia, Canada, and Alaska.[xlv] Thermokarst lakes are a result of abrupt thawing of permafrost, also a relatively new phenomenon. NASA recently released satellite videos showing a number of such lakes bubbling with methane that has been sequestered in the tundra for millennia. There are about 1,500 billion tons of carbon locked up in the world's Arctic tundra. As the tundra thaws, its carbon is released into the atmosphere as methane. Its release could significantly accelerate climate change, potentially triggering a runaway condition where increased arctic temperatures accelerate release of methane at an ever-increasing rate. Uncontrollable global warming would then cause major shifts in habitat for all life on Planet Earth, and potentially thaw the polar icecaps of Greenland and Antarctica, raising sea levels catastrophically. Referring to Rep. Schultz's quote above, release of methane from Arctic tundra is like steroids for the 800-pound gorilla. The warming trend in global climate must be reversed before the runaway condition is triggered. The fact that thermokarst lakes are already releasing significant methane from Arctic tundra means the mechanism that could trigger the runaway condition is already active.

Whether thawing tundra can somehow be controlled or reversed is a critical question. At the very least, methane emissions from arctic thermokarst lakes will make it much more challenging to keep average global temperature from rising above the 1.5 to 2.0 degrees C set by the international community. It will require cooperation and collective commitment beyond anything humanity has ever undertaken. There is no enemy and the main thing that needs to change is us. Anything less than our best will likely fall short.

Love and wisdom:

As noted previously, humanity has everything we need to reverse global climate change — if we act now! Even a coronavirus pandemic can have a silver lining; the world's emissions have slowed, while compassion and cooperation have been widely activated. Humanity must seize this momentum to more effectively address global climate change. There is always hope.

Domination Thinking

Many have become convinced that we must act in response to global warming and pollution, the resurgence in violence against racial and non-traditional gender minorities, and the ever-widening gap between the very rich and the multitude of poor people. It's wonderful that women are making strides toward workplace, education, and political equality with men, but the playing field remains far from level. It is only fear that makes men resist racial and gender equality and turn it into a struggle. The roll-back in environmental protection laws and funding, along with the ongoing marginalization of science, wildlife, and nature is very short-sighted. It makes no sense to think we must choose between the world's economy and nature's future capacity to support life! Our solutions must honor both.

That seems like plenty of problems, even though the list of things to fuss over could be longer. In a way, things are not as complicated as they seem. There is a single factor at the root of the entire mess humanity has made of our relationships with each other and Mother Earth — *Domination Thinking*. Merriam-Webster on-line dictionary defines *Domination* as "(1) supremacy or preeminence over another; (2) exercise of mastery or ruling power; (3) exercise of preponderant, governing or controlling influence."[xlvi] While mainly male in character, women are not immune from feeling the need to control life. Control via domination is driven by fear and lack of trust in each other and life. When I consider the problems humanity and Mother Earth share, I see domination thinking every time. It's not new. Genesis 1:26 (KJV) says God gave man "dominion over the earth," rather than responsibility to care for it. Millennia ago, its author had no way to foresee that dominion would one day threaten the world with destruction, but that's exactly what what's happening! Since the root behind domination thinking is fear, we need to stop being afraid, something that's often challenging. "How can I overcome being afraid of life?" is a powerful question. I've grown much from living with this question, and *Creation Is a Love Song* is a partial response. My understandings will continue to unfold so long as I live with the question.

It is vital that each of us live with this question until we find effective responses we can embrace. Your involvement matters because we will *never* see the future we desire, so long as our time and resources are focused on *dominating* our problems! We must take to heart Einstein's wisdom, "We cannot solve our problems with the same thinking we used when we created them." It truly is time for a shift to love and cooperation.

Love and wisdom:

For some time, I had been feeling pressure about my response to global climate change. Then during a guided meditation in March 2019, we were asked to write with our eyes closed, to help us stay focused on our inner voice. A verbatim quote of the wisdom I received is: "Love is who you are. The same is true for each person on Earth. That is all that matters. When you feel lost, relax and remember what you know about love. It is not your job to awaken the world. You are here to awaken Foster and share who you are. That will help others remember who they are." That fits me much better than trying to save the world.

CHAPTER 8
ACTING RESPONSIBLY

Interactions between Divinity and our conscious awareness are difficult to describe, even though inner wisdom, direct knowing, intuition, or implicit understanding have been guiding the shamans, seers, mystics, and prophets for most of human history. While it's hard to see labels like shaman or prophet fitting my self-image, divine inspiration and guidance were absolutely essential to writing the book you are holding. Such inner guidance has historically been ignored or actively debunked by science because it was considered inherently unverifiable, and therefore, impossible to confirm. Yet such inner guidance has been part of the human experience for millennia, sometimes with surprising outcomes. I believe neither science nor spirituality alone will guide humanity through the challenges we have created. Acting responsibly must include both ways of knowing in respectful balance as we move forward.

Science and Spirituality: Another Great Marriage

*"It is true that neither the ancient wisdoms nor the
modern sciences are complete in themselves.
They do not stand alone. They call for one another."*
— Thomas Merton, *I Have Seen what I was Looking for*

*"All matter originates and exists only by virtue of a force
which brings the particle of an atom to vibration and holds
this most minute solar system of the atom together. We must
assume behind this force the existence of a conscious and intel-
ligent Mind. This Mind is the matrix of all matter."*
— Max Planck, *The Nature of Matter*

The above quotes, the first from a spiritual mystic, the second from a from world-renowned physicist, recognize science and spirituality as two windows for viewing the same Universe. The two approaches use different methods (intuition vs. logic) and languages (words vs. mathematics), but they are addressing similar questions about the same Universe. Their approaches are so different, science and spirituality have often behaved as if they were two ancient rivals that forgot they have the same mother.

Spirituality has been part of human life since our early ancestors became aware of themselves and wondered, "Who / what am I?" or "Why am I here?" and "Does life have meaning?" Such questions have been the province of seers and mystics partly because they have been considered impossible to address using scientific methods. The search for meaning is a powerful driving force for those who seek clarity about their spiritual journey. There are many examples where mystical experiences have brought people deep meaning and clarity.

The earliest roots of science can be traced back to Ancient Egypt and Mesopotamia around 3000-3500 BCE,[xlvii] so it is also ancient. As an evidence-based way to view reality, science is anchored in verification by measurement. Its primary premise is to accept as true only that which has been repeatably confirmed by carefully controlled experiments. That restriction has benefitted humanity with many innovative technologies to control our surroundings, travel widely, and communicate globally. Science and spirituality have believed they were incompatible views of reality for centuries. That mutual exclusivity has begun to crumble.

Werner Heisenberg and Erwin Schrodinger independently observed in 1926, that light can behave as either a particle (photon) or wave. In fact, when matter is studied in its tiniest forms (atoms, subatomic particles, and light), classical physics is not adequate to describe its behavior. This led to the development of quantum physics, a theoretical science rooted in this dual nature of matter.

Classical physics beautifully describes the interactions between matter on a macro-scale. Everything from grains of sand to solar systems are *well-behaved*; their behavior fits the laws of classical physics. In quantum physics, results depended upon experimental conditions, including the observers (scientists) who were performing the experiments. The uncertainty of quantum physics was rejected by Einstein, who famously proclaimed, "God does not play dice with the Universe."[xlviii]

Despite its controversial beginning, quantum physics is becoming the bridge that reveals the long-hidden harmony between science and spirituality. Because words are such a clumsy tools, it's not easy to grasp, but when Gautama Buddha said, "With our thoughts, we make the world,"[xlix] and Jesus, the Christ taught, "Your faith has healed you *as you believe*,"[l] these avatars' words carry the same meaning as Schrodinger and Heisenberg demonstrating that the presence of an observer can alter experimental results. Don't worry if this rattles your sense of logic. But it is reassuring to me that applied kinesiology confirms the harmony between quantum physics and the avatars.

The marriage of science and spirituality is the coming together of two vastly different approaches for understanding reality. It's like the early stages of an arranged marriage between two people whose native culture and language are very different. Communicating is a big challenge and getting to know each other is in its early stages. The good news is they exist within the same reality. Their common drive to understand creation is destined to sustain the marriage until one day, the two shall become one.

Love and wisdom:

When the marriage of science and spirituality is fully realized, the following quote will come into full flower, "Someday, after mastering the winds, the waves, the tides, and gravity, we shall harness for God

the energies of love, and then, for the second time in the history of the world, man will have discovered fire."[ii] *(Pierre Teilhard de Chardin).*
Now is the time for humanity to harness the power of Love.

The Land of Alphabet Trees

Once we accept that Mother Earth and all who call her home are in a critical situation, it is obvious that we must unleash our creative energy to maximize our problem-solving results. As stated earlier, one reason *Creation Is a Love Song* was written is to awaken love for Mother Earth in the hearts of readers. A key aspect of our work is to shift humanity's modus operandi away from competition toward cooperation. Each of us must *choose* cooperation and love. Indeed, the shift Mother Earth requires of us will happen one person at a time. Love and cooperation, in combination with science, are the only viable pathway to a wholesome future for all of us. This is the time for each of us to set aside fear and listen to our higher instincts. Our relationships with Mother Earth and all life *really need* a revolutionary up-shift, in our individual and collective consciousness. That's why we're here!

I wrestled with a strong sense of urgency while writing *Creation Is a Love Song*. You'd think I would have learned by now that when I work with *over*-focused urgency on accomplishing any goal, my vision, creativity, output, and quality *decrease*. Yet, my urgency tries to push me there anyway. Having said that, it's a relief to be writing an essay called *The Land of Alphabet Trees*!

In group settings, there's plenty of evidence that a skilled facilitator using playful approaches, can open creative thinking and innovation beyond what strong focus and hard work could accomplish. Including variety in experience levels and functional expertise in playful problem-solving, teams can make them more effective and immune to group think. Don't be afraid to *color outside-the-lines* on this. For example, having a guest co-facilitator, like a grade school teacher or an improv comedian, could be a great addition.

On a Sunday morning several months ago, a group of friends were discussing ways to allow more joy and creativity into our lives. Noelle, an innovative fourth-grade teacher for twenty years, took us on a magic carpet ride to anyplace our imagination chose to take us. When the ride ended, we were asked to draw a picture of our surroundings or what it felt like to be there.

She was showing us how much fun being playful can be. I was pleasantly surprised that my rusty play gene kicked in so easily; I was a kid again in thirty seconds! My magic carpet took me to a land of rolling green hills with colorful scattered trees shaped like capital letters. My first name is Foster, so I sketched an 'F' tree. It was shaped like the letter with green bark and red leaves.

Noelle uses such techniques to make school fun for her students, while enhancing their imagination, confidence, and social skills. She has become masterful at integrating curriculum content into such playful exercises. Her students have fun in school while learning their lessons, almost without realizing it. I'm hopeful that Noelle represents a growing trend for education in America.

There is no question that fun enhances creativity, so it could be a big plus to allow more fun at work. If my retired-scientist mind can easily play like a kid, anyone can do it. It would make my heart sing to see fun-filled cooperation and creativity in the halls of corporations, education, and government across the world!

Love and wisdom:

Counterintuitive as it may seem in the midst of times that feel urgent, it is time to relax into a more loving and playful approach to life. Even in the midst of crises; even in the realms of business, education, and government; love, cooperation, and joy are not irresponsible! They are essential.

Reversing Global Warming

"The Chinese use two brush strokes to write the word 'crisis.' One brush stroke stands for danger; the other for opportunity. In a crisis, be aware of the danger — but recognize the opportunity."
— John F. Kennedy, 4/12/59

The decline in Mother Earth's capacity to sustain life is the biggest threat humanity has ever faced — and our greatest opportunity. The crisis demands that we fundamentally shift our long-held perceptions of human life, what is required of us, and how relationships work. These paradigm shifts are inner work assigned to all of us. If we fail to embody the required shifts, we face a future that feels like *hell on earth*. As the paradigm shifts are embraced by a critical portion of humanity, we will experience current global circumstances as an opportunity to create *heaven on earth*. The vast outer work of enacting our best efforts will flow from within as the paradigm shifts move into place. The choice we face is that stark: to let fear overwhelm us and accept hell on earth — or to be energized to create heaven on earth. The beliefs we choose determine our future.

Love and wisdom:

Embracing the paradigm shifts sets the stage for heaven on earth! What better reason could we have to move into relationships anchored in love? Just remember it happens from the inside out. We have the power and know-how to do this; it's why we're here.

Transforming Fear into Peace

Fear has been part of our psyche from humanity's earliest days. The natural world of our species' youth was wild and dangerous beyond our modern-day capacity to grasp. In the twenty-first century life is much safer, but our innate fear has not diminished in proportion. Love of power is an ego-driven reaction to fear. The ego's logic is "I won't have to fear circumstances that could harm me or those I love, if I amass the power to control them".

Many of us first encountered fear in early childhood from over-protective or indifferent parents. By the time many of us started school, fear was deeply embedded in our psyche. By the time we became adults, fear was locked in as an automatic reaction. In truth, most of the fearful things we imagine never happen. So, the mind's worry often has no basis. But fear-driven ego activity perpetuates the chaotic busyness of life anyway.

Many twenty-first century people are ensnared in a chaotic swirl, like some bizarre energy is pushing life in fearful directions. Fortunately, humans are born with the power to make our own choices, so we have the capacity to look our fears in the eye and *choose our response.* Life does not require that we allow fear to have dominion over us. In truth, feeling peaceful is about transcending one's fears, and has little to do with controlling the circumstances of life. To give up control is counterintuitive to our ego, yet we must trust life before our highest and best can freely flow to us. The surface chaos of life will be an ongoing treadmill so long as we try to alleviate fear by making external changes. Working to establish peace amongst our fellow humans won't be effective until we first allow peace to permeate our own inner being. The same is true for creating a peaceful relationship with Mother Earth. Trusting life, and its creator, is inner work that connects us to the deep reality within our own being.

Love and wisdom:

All peacemaking is an inside job first; the job belongs to each of us. Trusting life is the same as trusting God. And, we have everything we need to negotiate the peacemaking process — to the degree that we believe it lies within us. It really is done unto us as we believe! Like love and wisdom, faith and peace are a part of who we are. Our job is to accept the gift.

One Fundamental Paradigm Shift

When I read *Drawdown* and considered the many contributing factors to global climate change, reversing it seemed daunting. I was again reminded of Einstein's wisdom that problems cannot be solved with the same thinking used to create them. A paradigm shift is clearly needed. So, in addition to the complex list of tasks, we must prepare *ourselves* for the monumental work before us. Humanity needs an inner shift into harmony with Mother Earth so we can work together with nature to facilitate the flow of solutions.

It's easy to be confused by the many descriptions that have been used to express what this inner shift entails: move from suspicion to trust, exploitation to cooperation, *in*dependence *to inter*dependence, fear to love, etc. No matter how we express it, humanity is required to fundamentally shift how we think about life and our place in it. The alternative is a painful decline over the next few decades. The processes of global degradation are already underway, so time is important.

"When the Spirit is alive in people, they wake up from their mechanical thinking and enter the realm of co-creative power."
— Richard Rohr[lii]

Richard Rohr says it well. Once we awaken and transcend our mechanical thinking, co-creative power can flow through us. To thus awaken, humanity must learn to listen to our *heart* rather than our *head*. As humanity embraces this awakening, we will be much more adept at seeing our problems as opportunities, and effective in reversing global degradation and societal decline.

As noted in Chapter Five, human nature is anchored in fear. To usher in the new paradigm, we must overcome our fear-based, ego-centric human nature — fear can no longer be allowed to direct our responses to the circumstances we face. We are blessed that placing our heart's wisdom in charge does not require us to overcome or *kill* the ego; that's not even desirable. To shift away from ego control, we must make a conscious choice to place our ego in service to our soul/heart. Because your soul is born of God, it is the presence of love within you. So, the one fundamental paradigm shift required of humanity is to *move control of our marvelous Homo sapiens' brain from head (fear) to heart (love)*. It's like installing a new operating system.

The shift cannot be forced upon us by rules or legislation, nor can it happen en masse. It is, by its very nature, an individual choice. Only you can embrace that choice on your behalf. The paradigm shift will happen one heart and soul at a time.

Love and wisdom:

Reversing global degradation is within our capacities, or we would not have chosen to be on Earth at this critical time. Now is our moment to choose love. We didn't come here to hold a wake for Mother Earth!

Balance is Key

Moving through life with confidence and grace requires balance. When changes surprise us or fear knocks us off-balance, haste often feels essential. It is then wise to remember that hasty responses are much more likely to fall short of our best, or fail altogether. Because some facets of human behavior have been out of balance for millennia, the twenty-first century finds us facing challenges with time constraints that demand our urgent attention. Yet, if we hope to transcend our history and repair our relationships with each other and Mother Earth, we must establish balance as a species. For a few problems, now truly is the time to move quickly, but we must be sure our haste is buffered by awareness and wisdom. Moving fast can be dangerous if we lose our balance. Our urgent responses must unfold with clarity and confidence, rather than panic.

Finding and Keeping Our Balance

*"There is a collective force rising up on the earth today...
This is a time of a monumental shift, from the male dominance of human consciousness back to a balanced relationship between masculine and feminine."*
— Marianne Williamson, *A Woman's Worth*

It is critical that our relationship with the God of our understanding be in balance with its nature, because it shapes all our other relationships. The earliest religions were anchored in feminine ideas about the gods, perhaps because the mystery of new life manifested through women. Thus, the early gods had feminine characteristics; they were nurturing and provided for those who honored them. Although female ideas of the gods came first, the masculine desire for power has dominated human perceptions for the past few millennia. Masculine gods were strong, powerful beings who demanded loyalty in exchange for protection for those who honored them. To this day many people believe they are justified to make war upon other people that do not belong to their group, tribe, race, or nation. One could legitimately wonder if civilization has ever embraced a concept of divinity that carried feminine-masculine balance. In the opening two decades of the twenty-first century, human behavior clearly continues to favor masculine perceptions of God. But the anticipation is emerging that the Divine Feminine has begun to rise toward balance in our perceptions.

Of course, our collective understanding of God carries over into our relationships with each other and Mother Earth. Men have understood the biblical gift of dominion over the Earth to mean exploitation and domination, so those have been the prevailing paradigm for several thousand years. Had feminine ideals held sway, caring for strangers and nurturing Mother Earth might have become the norm, but that isn't what happened. So, we have long been fearful of *the other* and treated Planet Earth as in inanimate *thing* that exists for our benefit. In the past century, our demand for conveniences and comforts beyond basic needs has grown even more rapidly than our explosive growth in numbers. Humanity's resource consumption and thoughtless exploitation have thus grown exponentially far beyond what Mother Earth can sustain.

Our planet is a finite system that is incompatible with an ever-expanding economy and population. So long as human behavior is driven by fear and greed, over consumption will drag us ever deeper into unraveling Mother Earth's complex interdependent systems — the web of life.

Fear and greed often make people insistent, even belligerent, in defending their stance that there is no need to change our relationship with the planet. Over our long history on Planet Earth, humans have often found denial to be more comfortable than facing the need for change. Fear naturally results in blind spots.

Many people in the environmental movement have become equally entrenched in their position that change is essential in our relationship with Mother Earth. The heart-felt urgency on both sides has often resulted in tense confrontation. Such rigid opposing views naturally leave losers and winners scattered all over what has become a battlefield in a war of worldviews. Our relationships with Mother Earth have become quite sick while we find ourselves in a *war* over the symptoms. We are failing to address the root cause, partially because many people have yet to discern that there even is a root cause.

Of course, the infinite and loving energy field we call God has no gender and carries no masculine or feminine idea of itself. Humans have used our freedom of choice to select our beliefs, so our relationship with Planet Earth is distorted by our *perceptions* of God, not its *reality*. In that sense, we have *given ourselves* the right to do as we please with the planet. It is clear God does not need to change here. It is our *perceptions* of God that must shift into feminine-masculine balance. Because God *is* love, freeing ourselves from *domination thinking* would allow love to guide our relationships with ourselves, the rest of humanity, and Mother Earth.

When our collective relationship with God is thus refreshed, understanding dominion as rampant exploitation and unsustainable living will shift to embracing our responsibility as caretakers of a sustainable world. If this cradle of life is to continue supporting human presence here, we *must* insist on a healthy planet, and a world that works for everyone. Our economic and market-driven priorities must be brought into harmony with a healthy planet. In some sense, *Creation Is a Love Song* was born out of this confrontational dilemma.

Love and wisdom:

If Mother Earth is to sustain humanity into the deep future, we must embrace feminine — masculine balance and choose love as the foundation of all our relationships. As we rebalance our perceptions of God and embrace our role as caretakers of Mother Earth, a focused environmental movement will gradually fade as it becomes no longer necessary to enforce that which naturally unfolds.

What is Ours to Do?

This essay offers my thoughts on the basic question each of us faces: "What is mine to do?" The paradigm shift we have described as shifting toward love and away from fear is the same thing as increasing the collective consciousness of humanity. We can discuss what that means by using the ancient Hindu concept of Indra's net, a powerful model showing the interconnectedness of every element in all creation. Francis H. Cook, who wrote the book *Hua-Yen Buddhism: The Jewel Net of Indra,* describes this concept:

> ...in the heavenly abode of the great god Indra, there is a wonderful net which has been hung... in such a manner that it stretches out infinitely in all directions... [there is] hung a single glittering jewel in each "eye" of the net, and since the net itself is infinite in dimension, the jewels are infinite in number. There hang the jewels, glittering "like" stars in the first magnitude, a wonderful sight to behold. If we now arbitrarily select one of these jewels for inspection and look closely at it, we will discover that in its polished surface there are reflected *all* the other jewels in the net, infinite in number. Not only that, but each of the jewels reflected in this one jewel is also reflecting all the other jewels, so that there is an infinite reflecting process occurring. [liii]

If we confine our attention to the portion of Indra's Net associated with Planet Earth, and consider each jewel to be a specific piece of creation found here, we have married the idea of Indra's Net with the indigenous *web of life* described in the opening for Chapter One. Our Net has a jewel that represents each of us, along with everything else on Planet Earth. Each point is vibrating with energy exactly aligned with its consciousness.

"What is mine to do?" in support of moving from fear toward love now becomes clearer. We need to increase the energy of our vibration. How can we do that? Our life is a divine gift expressing itself as us, so we are *not* in a position to force its energy upward by our own effort. It is a matter of inviting divine love to draw us closer and daring to accept the divine gift. Our task is essentially one of *allowing* our energy of vibration to rise. This is inner work that belongs to all of us, individually and collectively. As humanity embraces this task, our individual and collective vibration (consciousness) will rise and contribute toward elevating the vibration of Indra's Net, as a whole. An avatar's vibration has the capacity to influence vast regions of Indra's Net, perhaps the whole thing. More ordinary people, like you and me, influence their immediate neighborhood of connections. But an increase in vibration of many thousands of ordinary people and small groups scattered about Indra's Net, can combine to increase the vibration (collective consciousness) of the whole enough to activate the paradigm shift.

We have described a paradigm shift as moving from away from fear toward love to make it more easily understood. The idea is sound because the vibration (consciousness) associated with love is remarkably more powerful than the energy of fear. This tremendous difference carries our hope of transcending the trends that are carrying life on Mother Earth toward misery and extinction. None of us can do it all; everyone is called to do their part.

Your contribution to the consciousness of humanity is terribly important to our collective future. That's why we're here! We don't have to figure out every detail before starting. Your soul already knows why it came here, so listen to your heart. One can grow in the direction of love one step at a time. The keys are to be willing and open. The flow of divine love that is expressing your life is overjoyed to inspire and guide your steps — all you have to do is remain willing and open.

Those who are uneasy because Indra's Net feels too intuitive might want to read *Power versus Force* by David R. Hawkins. You could combine his descriptions of consciousness with applied kinesiology to gain clarity on which steps would move you in the direction toward love. A simple question could be, "Would this step move me toward love?" Applied kinesiology can tell you "yes" or "no."

CHAPTER 9
AN EVEN BIGGER PICTURE

Lahokam is the name of the soul that enlivens this life as Foster. The essays collected in Chapter 9 describe my understanding of Lahokam's destiny. Humanity's shared history with Mother Earth is indeed beyond our comprehension. At the same time, Earth is only a tiny piece of creation. The Universe is an infinity of individual expressions of creation, each with a name that is known to the mind of God. Physical creation has been called the body of God.

All this vastness is the context for life. There are unnumbered places besides Earth that hold wonders beyond our imagination. In that bigger picture, the whole litany of *problems* this book has highlighted can be seen as opportunities for soul evolution. This offers us perspective about the feeling of urgency associated with our current crises here. We are not responsible for creation. We are not accountable to preserve or sustain all life. We are here on Earth to evolve as souls by doing our best with the opportunities we have been given. Within our collective potential, we have the capacity to resolve the whole mess we have made of Planet Earth. That is how soul evolution works. We are intended to encounter situations that stretch us into our potential. Soul evolution *requires* such opportunities (problems).

We don't have to grasp or figure out how to handle all of it. Each of us is called only to do our part the best we can, moment by moment. Perfection is not required of us; just our best. Neither do we have to understand it all. We cannot control the collective flow of creative events unleashed by our individual responses to the opportunities we encounter. Our choice is to trust that the flow of life on Earth will continue.

We can be secure in knowing we have done our part to the best of our ability. God caresses Mother Earth within its presence, the same presence that holds each of our lives and all creation. As Einstein said, we can only stand in awe and bow our heads.

Every Soul's Quest is Its Destiny

"No one saves us but ourselves. No one can and no one may. We ourselves must walk the path."
— Gautama Buddha, *The Dharma*

Despite our oneness during this lifetime, Foster's destiny is not the same as Lahokam's. This truth is similar for all of us. First of all, this life as Foster will end at my death; Lahokam's life goes on and on. The freedom of choice inherent in being human means none of us began this life with a predetermined destiny. You can't have a predetermined destiny *and* freedom of choice. A person's life pathway and final outcomes are shaped by living it. The choices made, reasons for making them, their consequences, and the lessons learned are how earthly life experiences support a soul's evolution. So, although a soul comes into a human incarnation with some intentions for that life, those intentions are not its destiny, or the destiny of its Homo sapiens host. A soul's long life goes on and on along a unique pathway that is shaped by uncountable experiences across hundreds, perhaps thousands, of incarnations. While a soul's pathway is thus unique, the same destiny is assured for every soul in the Cosmos.

Before entering a particular incarnation, a soul reviews the various potential pathways for that life's unfoldment; one of which is understood to be the most optimum.[liv] Its choice to participate in that life carries the optimum pathway as its set of intentions for that life. But, the human blend of soul and body has the option to accept or deny that intended life flow at every fork in the pathway. That looks a whole lot like a person choosing to accept or deny their destiny, but as pointed out, we humans don't have one. In comparison, souls do have a destiny that unfolds over many human incarnations and myriad other experiences. And, that overall soul destiny is assured by a sacred process of evolution that cannot be denied.

Our soul's origin is lost from memory across untold time and distance. But there was a moment when our soul's life and light emerged as a spark from within Divinity itself, by a birth process we don't understand and can't describe. That infant soul was nurtured and sustained in a soul nursery until it was ready to join other adolescent souls in a soul group meant to facilitate growth toward their destiny. It is a gentle love-filled process with no pressure or expectations exerted upon the soul, except those that are self-generated by its own eagerness to grow. At a point when its soul guide (mentor) and the soul agree, an opportunity for its first incarnation will arise.[lv]

To explain what happens when a soul begins evolving toward its destiny, consider climbing a mountain as a metaphor. Every soul is climbing the same mountain. All of them have the same quest; to reach the destiny that awaits them at the summit. The mountain has as many pathways as there are souls climbing, so no two souls have identical journeys. Each soul shapes its path, choice by choice, as its journey proceeds over many incarnations and other experiences in the non-physical realms. Some paths turn out to be very challenging, others are easier. Some turn out to be very long; others are more direct. Choices are in play the whole journey, so the variety of soul journeys is unimaginable. The journey is so complex and challenging that hundreds of incarnations and innumerable other non-physical adventures are needed before a soul finally reaches the summit. We can't even imagine the vastness or rigors of a soul journey, yet a soul never questions the value of its journey or its destination. The Divine One that birthed them long ago waits at the summit. There are an unfathomable number of souls, but only one destiny. From the moment each soul was born from within Divinity itself, it has had the purpose and destiny to rejoin the source from which it arose. None can wander off the mountain, even though we sometimes feel lost. A soul's quest and its destiny are the same; reunion with God. They have eternity to work with and every soul completes its journey.

Why is Life Designed to Work as it Does?

We are trying to peek into the mind of God here, but intuition has provided a response confirmed by applied kinesiology. I offer it as a possibility. Without physical creation there was only oneness, so the physical realms came into being so God could experience itself and have a universe full of beings with whom to share relationships. God may have many reasons for continually creating souls, but their nature clearly provides the opportunity for growth. The long arc of a soul's life begins and ends in God, but during its long life, it expands its love, beauty, and power many times over by the time it rejoins the One. This is a mechanism by which God continues to expand into its own potential over the eons. As we grow in wisdom and love over our lifetime, that process contributes to the expansion of God itself. As noted earlier, how an infinite being can also keep expanding is a mystery, I have no way to address. But neither does it make sense to think an infinite God has some type of limiting boundary. So, I choose to believe God continually expands by experiencing itself through its own creation.

Love and wisdom:

That's how precious creation and each of us are! The implications of this hypothesis are staggering! Because human beings are part of God, we have no limitations except those we impose on ourselves. As beings with freedom of choice, we always have the power to change our life by changing our thinking

Our Greatest Opportunity

"Love is our true destiny."
— Thomas Merton, *Love and Living*

How does this picture of soul life and purpose relate with our current situation here on Earth? Humanity has been trapped for millennia in ever-repeating cycles of creating our own problems and then trying to solve them with the same level of thinking we used to create them. So, it is not surprising that the great opportunity we share in the twenty-first century is to raise our individual and collective consciousness. Enhancing consciousness is the path to move out of our habitual thought patterns toward lasting solutions. Then we will be able to effectively address global warming and the other maladies we have created. To help make this clear, the definition given below is what I mean by *consciousness* in the context of this discussion. Expanding our consciousness is exactly the same thing as soul evolution.

Consciousness is a state of inner awareness that determines how we see ourselves, our relationships, and our thoughts about how life works. Everyone's experience of life is shaped by their consciousness.
— Foster Harding and Cindy Harlan[lvi]

Love and wisdom:

Enhanced consciousness allows us to see Mother Earth's problems within a much larger context, which makes them less overwhelming and more approachable.

Our experience of life tends to unfold in harmony with our expectations, so if we fear life, our acts tend to result in reasons to fear life, and we experience a downward spiral. Fear clogs our efforts with doubts, judgements, and blame. Similarly, if we trust life, our efforts tend to result in reasons to trust life, and we experience an upward spiral. It seems we must trust life before we can act with any effectiveness at all. But how do we learn that life can be trusted?

In the First Epistle of John, we are told that God is Love.

"He that does not love does not know God; for God is love."
— I John 4:8[lvii]

Love and wisdom:

Does believing that God is love help us trust life? When we remember that our soul was born an individual child of God, trusting life is as natural as your next breath. We are then free to grow into our full potential.

Going Deeper

Autobiography of a Yogi is Paramahansa Yogananda's story of how he came to know himself as an "Incarnation of Love." I have known for several years that I came into this life to *be* love, but what that means is far more than I had realized. The Yogi's realization of love (God) seems light years beyond my own. With nearly eight decades already behind me, it is not possible to become a young man and travel to India seeking a guru. It seems impossible to approach Yogananda's level of enlightened awareness in this lifetime. I cannot follow his path. What to do?

Shortly after the question arose, meditation revealed a path forward. For the rest of this life as Foster, I am to trust my soul, Lahokam, as my guru. I don't know how far I can travel in the direction of love (God)-realization in this lifetime, but in this life as Foster, Lahokam has already expanded far beyond any of its prior incarnations. My soul-calling for this lifetime has always been to travel as far as possible in the direction of love. So, as long as I have breath, divine love will continue calling me toward reunion with itself. Love is the engine that drives the eternal cycles of creation. That is true for all of us.

The Deep Future is Unbounded

Everything, from a subatomic particle to a universe, has its unique vibration, including each of us. As noted earlier, every locus of energy in the infinity of creation contributes its vibration to the Net of Indra. Hindu holy men say that all of these combined vibrations are the voice of God; the holy word, *Aum*.[lviii] This word is also frequently spelled Om or Ohm. Its use is still common today in the Hindu and Buddhist traditions as part of songs and chants. All the vibrations of creation were contained in the word (*Aum*) and once it was spoken, it has been reverberating as creation ever since. Yogananda said it is not unusual for a fully realized human (yogi) to actually hear the sound of *Aum* when in deep meditation. When that happens John 1:1, 3 (NJV) becomes literal truth. I will state it from a yogi's perspective; "In the beginning was *Aum*, and *Aum* was with God, and *Aum* was God. All things were made by him; and without him was not any thing made that was made." It bears repeating that God has no aspect of gender associated with its character. Our use of language often assigns masculine pronouns to God. That has no anchor at all in God's reality. God is love. My heart is certain that *Aum* is the vibration of love.

As I awoke on a recent morning, a realization came as a blissful feeling beyond description. It is the destiny of *my* soul, Lahokam, to experience infinity by reuniting with God. It's true for Lahokam, as well as in general. The realms of a soul's vast lifetime on the way to that moment of reuniting are arrayed as stages of evolution in spiritual consciousness powered by divine love. Earthly language attempts to describe some of our future stages as ascended masters, soul guides, angels, archangels, and yes, gods. All of this potential lies within our soul destiny. The sum total of who we are, and where we are going, is love. This morning I sensed the soul Lahokam, the one who animates this life as Foster, expanding into ever-more powerful expressions of love. We all are destined to become one with God. When or how that happens matters not. It is encoded in our spiritual DNA. Our destiny is certain. We *are* love — and beyond...

Love Song – The Elder

All the song ever
asked me to sing
are the notes of love
offered me each day —
and trust, that all
together, they are
the love song I was
born to sing.

— Foster Laverne Harding

THE COVID-19 PANDEMIC

What can an author say about a public health disaster of this magnitude, especially in the context of *Creation Is a Love Song*? After all, I have proclaimed that creation actually is a love song, continually emerging from a caring and benevolent God. Has the COVID-19 pandemic somehow altered the nature of God, negating the Bible's recognition that God is love, or has it placed limitations on that concept's validity?

To be sure, it is hard to see how such levels of human suffering, with so many people dying, could be consistent with a loving, benevolent God. Is it possible to reconcile such contrasts through a current perspective? Or, are we being asked to live with the tension and allow our questions to guide us to deeper love and commitment to serving the world? This question applies equally well to the other divides and challenges our world is facing. How are we to respond to such tumultuous times?!

There is no need to repeat the broadly-communicated details of the virus, or the powerful impacts the pandemic has brought to human life across today's global village. We have been shaken. My intuition says this pandemic may adversely affect more people than anything since WWII.

The COVID-19 pandemic has often been compared to the Spanish flu pandemic. A century ago, it is estimated to have infected 500 million people, a third of the world's population at the time. Total estimated world-wide deaths attributed to the Spanish flu range from 17 to 100 million. The uncertainty of the range is due to widespread censorship associated with WWI, along with much less connected world communications a century ago. In any case, total cases and resulting deaths from COVID-19 are, so far, much lower. That does not necessarily imply that COVID-19 is a more benign or less contagious disease. There were no vaccines for the Spanish flu. Antibiotics, steroids, respiratory ventilators, and other modern-day medical tools and procedures were also decades in the future at that time. Comparing then to now, medical knowledge, technology, and communications have all become vastly more advanced. I conclude, despite the staggering impacts of COVID-19, that this is the best time in history for humanity to endure such a pandemic.

Innovations in medical science have also revealed improved vaccine technology and other medical advances throughout our response to COVID-19. That progress will very likely continue, so whenever the next pandemic shows up, that future time will be the new best time in human history for it to happen. It seems there is a wave-front of advancing capabilities, medical and otherwise, that accompany humanity on our travels through time. I believe this observation operates in parallel with, and is rooted in, the soul evolution that characterizes earthly life.

However, as this book emphasizes, Mother Earth's natural world is the only context ever known, available now, or for the foreseeable future, where Homo sapiens naturally thrive. It is imperative that humanity respect Mother Earth's requirements as we move forward in harmony with *her* needs!

What began as an outbreak of the virus in the city of Wuhan, China took a while to be recognized as a threat to the rest of the world. Many governments failed to anticipate what was coming or how rapidly it would spread. Much of the world rapidly shifted from mild interest in a far-off event, to panic at the rapid spread and deadly nature of COVID-19.

The story of my personal experience begins when my wife and I had gathered with friends in southwest Florida for some sunshine and warmth in late February of 2020. While there, concern ramped up significantly as news media and the public awakened to what was happening and how threatening it could become. In early March, on the day of our return flight from Ft. Meyers, the city announced their first death from COVID-19. Upon our return, we chose to minimize contact with people for the next two weeks in case we had contracted the disease. But we made exceptions, because we still didn't recognize how widespread and deadly COVID-19 would become. By mid-March, the State of Colorado announced their first lockdown. Marilyn and I went from experiencing a low level of concern about flying to Florida to being in lockdown within the space of just three weeks!

Personal fear quickly arose with the lockdown; at seventy-eight with diabetes, I was at high-risk for serious consequences if I caught the virus. Caution rose in parallel with fear. It felt like death was stalking me, and I could die if it successfully caught up. Staying isolated felt like the only choice for both of us. I also found that fear in one area of life was soon permeating the rest. After a while, I was driving slower and being more rigorous about locking both our house and my car. On those few occasions when it was essential to visit the grocery store or pharmacy, I was really tense. Then upon reentering our house, there was a strong sense of relief. Not necessarily logical; I could have been carrying the disease home with me!

The months dragged on and on and 2020 ended with little change in outlook. Vaccines were just gaining emergency use approval by the United States FDA (Food and Drug Administration). At the time of this writing in February 2021, despite wide-spread emergency use, they are not yet fully approved by the United States FDA. Furthermore, vaccinating enough people across the world to effectively end the pandemic will take most of 2021 under optimistic scenarios. As seems to happen with almost every issue in US culture, politicizing of the pandemic became a depressing side note. Sadly, the pandemic seemed to highlight and magnify the divisions in several facets of our society, far beyond politics.

Video conferencing became the safest way to see our friends and family. As an affectionate man, who for years has specialized in big hugs, video was pretty lukewarm, but admittedly better than no visual contact. Email, phone conversations, and texts are not very effective for me. I don't hear well over the phone and typing/reading text is fraught with errors, misunderstandings, and false impressions. Many have said 2020 was the longest year they had ever experienced; I have to concur.

In addition, my connection with our local spiritual community atrophied with suspension of in-person activities. My heart remains invested there, but it has felt disconnected and distant. A nice array of video activities came along after a few months, but participating depressed me. It is painful to have my love stoked by video contact and have no way to adequately express my feelings. For me, it's been more comfortable not to participate and leave my emotions more or less dormant. Stuck in the semi-comfort of my self-imposed isolation, I hadn't realized my absence had an impact on our community, until one of our closest friends called it to my attention. I now realize my friends and loved ones are worthy of more from me than dropping out, so my response to COVID-19 remains a work in progress. I have no way to know how the COVID-19 pandemic has impacted readers of *Creation Is a Love Song*, but I hope its effects have been tempered by recognizing the good that also inherently accompanies all of life's experiences.

I'm happy to say the pandemic has brought silver linings. The lack of activities, accompanied by feelings of boredom, offered both opportunity and incentive to complete and publish *Creation Is a Love Song*. That's something about the pandemic for which I'm grateful. Another has been our emerging connection with the

Findhorn eco-village/spiritual community in northern Scotland. Discovering, and participating in, three video workshops and other activities, allowed us to appreciate Findhorn in tangible ways, not just as a conceptual idea. We have been lifted up and are grateful that our deeper connection nurtured meaningful spiritual growth.

At last, in February of 2021, Marilyn and I are scheduled to receive our two COVID-19 vaccine shots. Caution will remain necessary for months to come, but it brings a strong sense of relief that COVID-19 will no longer feel life-threatening. Our daily lives may not change as quickly as we'd like, but the vaccine offers relief and hope that a bright future will unfold over the coming months. I am certain we will appreciate life more than ever.

Has there been a spiritual side to my COVID-19 experience, something associated with deeper meaning? Yes! It has strongly reinforced an already deep sense of calling to support the paradigm shift toward love. That's what this book and my life are about.

Now to the question: "Why did humanity have to suffer the COVID-19 pandemic?" While it is not likely that science will ever prove direct cause and effect, I firmly believe the COVID-19 pandemic arose from the imbalances we have brought to the web of life on Planet Earth. In that sense, responsibility for the pandemic is shared by most of humanity. Because I trust God and life, I simply can't see the COVID-19 tragedy as a divinely sanctioned event, sent to punish us by an angry, vengeful God. It would be against the laws of its nature for a God of love to be divided against itself in such ways. Instead, I believe the pandemic arose as a result of normal cause and effect. It is a natural event unfolding within the context of natural laws, just like gravity, weather, or the seasons. There is no-one and nothing to blame. We are simply experiencing the consequences of our own out-of-balance behaviors over the generations.

We had no way to know, but our world-view, our understanding of how life works, has been too human-centered and thus out of balance with Mother Earth's needs — for the past few millennia! In that sense, the pandemic has brought a clear message for us to see and respond to. It's time for us to shift into harmony with the rest of creation and align with her natural laws. The further out of balance we live in relation to creation's natural laws, the more severe the consequences we encounter.

Our actions also bring the same consequences to Mother Earth and all life here. I pray that humanity will have the wisdom to see this truth, and the courage to cooperate effectively, as we move forward. Mother Earth urgently needs our help if she is to continue supporting life as we know it. It could be a long walk for humanity before we are out of the woods.

Although we are God's children, it is not God's job to fix our mistakes. God is not that kind of parent. If that was God's job, the results of our actions couldn't bring the consequences, lessons, and soul evolution we came here to experience. Remember, Earth is an experiential school for souls. Creation is the love song of the creator; how we care for creation is up to humanity. God is by nature found within our own being. So, we are assured that God is with us, no matter what problems we create.

For me, the pandemic has reinforced the wake-up call already present in my awareness from global climate change and accelerated species extinction. I am grateful for the added power of an in-our-face reminder that we need to mend our ways — now is the time.

Soli Deo Gloria!

Acknowledgments

All of us live within the River of Life that began expressing on this planet eons ago. We evolved within it and all of it is part of us. As a human being, I am indebted to all my ancestors and every fragment of life that preceded me or shares this life today. We can say, along with each prior generation, "This is our time to shine." So, I am grateful for the flow of life that brought all of us to this momentous time in the life of Mother Earth.

As an author, I am grateful for ideas, language to express them, and those who shaped our physical and spiritual heritage over many millennia. Particular thanks are offered to the avatars, saints, seers, scientists, skeptics, teachers, and students whose ideas and revelations have blessed us through the ages.

I write for the joy of exploring life experiences and bringing to light the lessons they contain. Interest in publishing, sales, and marketing has always felt secondary to my love of nature and the quest to understand life. But being a *bringer of the light* can be a fruitless, frustrating adventure if no-one is aware of the gifts you hope to share with the world. Without help from lots of loving, wise, and helpful people, the light I hoped to share would have remained *under a bushel* and lost. Deep thanks to all my teachers and mentors.

Especially, love and thanks to my wife Marilyn. We have shared many of our adventures and her generous heart has gracefully supported the second half of life. I am so grateful for her loving presence! Good friends Steve Poos-Benson and Paige Prendergast read early drafts and offered sorely needed support and insights. Love you guys! Patti Hostetler and Amy Graziano at Douglas Land Conservancy kindly placed several articles in their monthly newsletter based on essays that became part of *Creation Is a Love Song*. Thank you for building my confidence! To the ministers, practitioners, and congregants at the Center for Spiritual Living Castle Rock: Thank you for helping me become a spiritual teacher.

My editor AnnaBeth Davidson was recommended by a friend. She proved to be a true professional in all aspects of editing the book. She also brought unexpected blessings by helping me be a better writer. Her suggestions that I bring more sensory content into scenes and events added depth and meaning to help you, dear readers, stay engaged with the book. Thank you, AnnaBeth!

My long-time friend Barbara Lane designed the book cover and created my blog page and website, https://www.FosterHarding.com. Thank you! She also introduced me to Crystal Blue, who recommended a team of Victoria Wolf and Camille Parker to move the manuscript from final draft to finished product. Without these four, the book you are holding would never have found its way into your hands. I am grateful. I am grateful for so many others who helped bring *Creation Is a Love Song* into the light! Your names are in my heart.

Last and foremost, I express deep gratitude for guidance and inspiration from my indwelling soul. In a process that is still ongoing, this soul has shaped who I am as a human being. *Creation Is a Love Song* flowed into existence via that inner voice. I am grateful until my final exhale. When this life as Foster ends, my soul will again become undiluted wholeness. Life and love just keep going and expanding. Eternal gratitude for creation and Creator!

BIBLIOGRAPHY

Books

Born, Max, Albert Einstein, Irene Born, trans., *The Born-Einstein Letters,* New York: Macmillan Press Ltd., 1971, 2005.

Brown, Tom, Jr. *Grandfather.* New York: Berkley Books, 1993.

Byrom, Thomas. *Dhammapada: The Sayings of the Buddha.* Boston, MA: Shambhala Publications Inc., 1976

Caddy, Eileen. *Opening Doors Within.* Rochester, VT: Findhorn Press, 2019.

Cook, Frances H. *Hua-Yen Buddhism: The Jewel Net of Indra.* University Park, PA: The Pennsylvania State University, 1977

Devorkin, David H., and Robert W. Smith. *The Hubble Cosmos.* Washington, DC: National Geographic, 2015

Eiseley, Loren. *The Immense Journey: An Imaginative Naturalist Explores the Mysteries of Man and Nature.* New York: Vintage Books, 1959.

Emoto, Masuro. *The Secret Life of Water.* New York: Atria Books, 2005.

Haich, Elizabeth. *Initiation.* Santa Fe, NM: Aurora Press, 2000. Kindle Book

Harding, Foster Laverne. *The Great University of Life.* Golden, CO: Park Point Press, 2013.

Hawken, Paul, ed. *Drawdown: The Most Comprehensive Plan Ever Proposed to Reverse Global Warming.* New York: Penguin Books, 2017.
   —*The Magic of Findhorn.* New York: Bantam Books, 1975.

Hawking, Stephen. *A Brief History of Time.* New York: Bantam Books, 1996.

Hawkins, David R. *Power versus Force.* Carlsbad, CA: Hay House, 2002.

Lamsa, George. *Holy Bible: From the Ancient Eastern Text.* New York: A.J. Holman Co., 1933
—*Jesus, the Christ, The Holy Bible from the Ancient Eastern Text.* San Francisco CA: Harper, 1968.

Mann, Charles C. *1491, New Revelations of the Americas Before Columbus.* New York: Vintage Books 2005.
—*1493: Uncovering the New World Columbus Created.* New York: Vintage Books, 2011.

Neihardt, John G. *Black Elk Speaks.* Lincoln, NE: Univ. of Nebraska Press, 2014.

Newton, Michael. *Destiny of Souls.* St. Paul, MN: Llewellyn, 2006.
—*Journey of Souls.* St. Paul, MN: Llewellyn, 2003.

Regan, Lilith. *Quotes by Pierre Teilhard de Chardin: The Complete Collection of Over 100 Quotes.* Independently published, 2020

Teilhard de Chardin, Pierre, René Hague, trans. *Toward the Future.* London: William Collins & Sons Ltd., Harcourt Inc., 1975.

Yogananda, Paramahansa. *Autobiography of a Yogi.* Los Angeles, CA: Self-Realization Fellowship, 2007.

Articles and Digital Sources

Adams, Jay, "'Thinking Big' about the future of the High Line Canal," *Denver Water,* April 9, 2018, https://www.denverwater. org/tap/thinking-big-about-the-future-of-the-high-line-canal

Barrett Oden, Loretta, "Cultural cooking: Acclaimed Potawatomi chef Loretta Barrett Oden finds inspiration in her roots," *Citizen Potawatomi Nation,* accessed 3/29/21 https:// www.potawatomi.org/cultural-cooking-acclaimed-potawatomi-chef-loretta-barrett-oden-finds-inspiration-roots/

"Chicxulub Crater," *Wikipedia,* accessed 3/29/21, https:// en.wikipedia.org/wiki/Chicxulub_crater

"Crow Indian Reservation," *Wikipedia*, accessed 3/29/21, http://en.wikipedia.org/wiki/Crow_Indian_Reservation

"Domination," *Merriam-Webster Online,* accessed 3/29/21, https://www.merriam-webster.com/dictionary/domination

Harding, Foster Laverne, Cindy Harlan. Speech presented at Sacred Community Circle, Castle Rock, CO, December 2019.

"High Line Canal Vision Statement," *High Line Canal Conservancy,* accessed 3/29/21, https://highlinecanal.org/vision/

"History of Science," *Wikipedia,* accessed 3/29/21, https://
en.wikipedia.org/wiki/History_of_Science

"Implied Contract," *Law.com: Legal Dictionary,*
accessed 3/29/21, https://dictionary.law.com/Default.
aspx?selected=905

"Implied-in-fact Contract," *Wikipedia,* accessed 3/29/21,
https://en.wikipedia.org/wiki/Implied-in-fact_contract

Jemison, Peter, "Restoring Our Food and Culture Through
the Natural World." Speech presented at the Seneca Art and
Cultural Center, Victor, NY, October 27, 2019.

"Kinesiology," *Wikipedia,* accessed 3/29/21, https://en.wikipe-
dia.org/wiki/Kinesiology.

"Mary Jemison," *Wikipedia,* accessed 3/29/21, https://en.wiki-
pedia.org/wiki/Mary_Jemison

"New Genome Comparison Finds Chimps, Humans Very
Similar at the DNA Level," *NIH: National Human Genome
Research Institute,* updated March 12, 2012, https://www.
genome.gov/15515096

Osborne, Hannah, "NASA Has Discovered Arctic Lakes
Bubbling with Methane – and That's Very Bad News,"

Newsweek, September 13, 2018, https://www.newsweek.com/
arctic-permafrost-lakes-bubbling-methane-nasa-1119624

"Peace Treaty Pageant," *Peace Treaty,* accessed 3/29/21, https://
peacetreaty.org/events/pageant/

Rohr, Richard. " Creation Reflects God's Glory," *Center for
Action and Contemplation,* February 18, 2018, https://cac.org/
creation-reflects-gods-glory-2018-02-18/
    —"The Shape of the Universe is Love," *Center for Action
and Contemplation,* February 29, 2016, https://cac.org/
the-shape-of-the-universe-is-love-2016-02-29/

    —"Cultivation Not Domination," *Center for Action
and Contemplation,* May 19, 2020, https://cac.org/
cultivation-not-domination-2020-05-19/

"Seneca Art and Cultural Center," *Ganondagan,* accessed
3/29/21, https://www.ganondagan.org/sacc

Stokes, John, trans., et al., "Haudenosaunee Thanksgiving
Address," *National Museum of the American Indian,* accessed
3/29/21, https://americanindian.si.edu/environment/
pdf/01_02_Thanksgiving_Address.pdf

Wall Kimmerer, Robin, "Restoring Our Food and Culture
Through the Natural World." Speech presented at the Seneca Art

and Cultural Center, Victor, NY, October 27, 2019.

"What is AK?" *ICAK-USA,* accessed 3/9/2021, https://www.icakusa.com/what-is-ak.

"What is the Universe Made Of?" *National Aeronautics and Space Administration,* accessed 3/29/21, https://wmap.gsfc.nasa.gov/universe/uni_matter.html

Endnotes

i   "Kinesiology," Wikipedia, https://en.wikipedia.org/wiki/Kinesiology

ii   "What is AK?" ICAK-USA, https://www.icakusa.com/what-is-ak

iii   David R. Hawkins, Power v.s. Force, pages 2-7

iv   David R. Hawkins, Power v.s. Force, pages 55-66

v   Michael Newton, Journey of Souls, 263-272

vi   Richard Rohr, "Creation Reflects God's Glory:" https://cac.org/creation-reflects-gods-glory-2018-02-18/

vii   Charles C. Mann, 1493: Uncovering the New World Columbus Created

viii   John G. Neihardt, Black Elk Speaks, Being the Life Story of a Holy Man of the Oglala Sioux, pages 88-89

ix   Charles C. Mann, 1491, New Revelations of the Americas Before Columbus, 110-115

x   ibid, pg. 363

xi   "Crow Indian Reservation," Wikipedia, http://en.wiki-pedia.org/wiki/Crow_Indian_Reservation

xii   "Mary Jemison," Wikipedia, https://en.wikipedia.org/wiki/Mary_Jemison

xiii   Seneca Art and Cultural Center, https://www.ganon-dagan.org/sacc

xiv   Peter Jemison, speech given 10/27/19, Restoring Our Food and Culture Through the Natural World, Seneca Art and Cultural Center, https://www.ganondagan.org/sacc

xv   ibid

xvi   John Stokes, trans., et al. "Haudenosaunee Thanksgiving Address" https://americanindian.si.edu/environment/pdf/01_02_Thanksgiving_Address.pdf

xvii   Robin Wall Kimmerer, speech given 10/27/19, Restoring Our Food and Culture Through the Natural World, Seneca Art and Cultural Center, https://www.ganondagan.org/sacc

xviii   Loretta Barrett Oden, Citizen Potawatomi Nation, https://www.potawatomi.org/cultural-cooking-ac-claimed-potawatomi-chef-loretta-barrett-oden-finds-in-spiration-roots/

xix   "Chicxulub Crater," Wikipedia, https://en.wikipedia.org/wiki/Chicxulub_crater

xx   NASA, What is the Universe Made of, https://wmap.gsfc.nasa.gov/universe/uni_matter.html

xxi   George Lamsa, Holy Bible From the Ancient Eastern

Text, 1 John 4:8

xxii   Lilith Regan, Quotes by Pierre Telihard de Chardin: The Complete Collection of Over 100 Quotes

xxiii   Richard Rohr, "The Shape of the Universe is Love," https://cac.org/the-shape-of-the-universe-is-love-2016-02-29/

xxiv   Masuro Emoto, The Secret Life of Water, pages 143-178

xxv   Tom Brown, Jr., Grandfather

xxvi   Loren Eisley, The Immense Journey, page 15

xxvii   Foster Harding, The Great University of Life, Chapter 1

xxviii   "Peace Treaty Pagent," Peace Treaty, http://peacetreaty.org/events/pageant

xxix   David H. Devorkin and Robert W. Smith, The Hubble Cosmos, pages 189, 115-118, 109

xxx   NASA, What is the Universe Made of, https://wmap.gsfc.nasa.gov/universe/uni_matter.html

xxxi   David H. Devorkin and Robert W. Smith, The Hubble Cosmos, pages 108-111

xxxii   Stephen Hawking, A Brief History of Time, Chapter 12—Conclusion

xxxiii   Elizabeth Haich, Initiation, chapters 20 & 26

xxxiv   "New Genome Comparison Finds Chimps, Humans Very Similar at the DNA Level," NIH: National Human Genome Research Institute, https://www.genome.gov/15515096

xxxv   Foster Laverne Harding, The Great University of Life, Chapter 6

xxxvi   Michael Newton, Destiny of Souls, page 1

xxxvii   Michael Newton, Journey of Souls, pages 13-16

xxxviii   Jay Adams, "Thinking Big about the future of The Highline Canal," https://www.denverwater.org/tap/thinking-big-about-the-future-of-the-high-line-canal

xxxix   "Implied Contract," Law.com: Legal Dictionary, https://dictionary.law.com/Default.aspx?selected=905

xl   "Implied-in-fact Contract," Wikipedia, https://en.wikipedia.org/wiki/implied-in-fact-contract/

xli   "Highline Canal Vision Statement," High Line Canal Conservancy, https://highlinecanal.org/vision/

xlii   Paul Hawken, The Magic of Findhorn

xliii   Hannah Osborne, Newsweek, "NASA Has Discovered Arctic Lakes Bubbling with Methane – and That's Very Bad News," https://www.newsweek.com/arctic-permafrost-lakes-bubbling-methane-nasa-1119624

xliv   Paul Hawken ed., Drawdown, page 220

xlv   Ibid.

xlvi   "Domination," Merriman-Webster On-line Dictionary, https://www.merriamwebster.com/dictionary/domination

xlvii   "History of Science," Wikipedia, https://en.wikipedia.org/wiki/History_of_Science

xlviii   Max Born, Albert Einstein, Irene Born trans., "Letter to Max Born, 1926," The Born-Einstein Letters

xlix   Thomas Byrom, Dhammapada: The Sayings of Buddha

l   George M Lamsa, trans. Jesus the Christ, Luke 17:19 & 18:42

li   Pierre Teilhard de Chardin, Toward the Future

lii   Richard Rohr, Daily Meditation Email, May 19,2020

liii   Frances H. Cook, Hua-Yen Buddhism: The Jewel Net of Indra, page 2

liv   Michael Newton, Destiny of Souls pages 355-357

lv   Ibid. pages 125-133

lvi   Foster Harding and Cindy Harlan, talk given 12/2019

lvii   George M Lamsa, trans., Jesus the Christ

lviii   Paramahansa Yogananda, Autobiography of a Yogi, page 128, footnote

Made in the USA
Middletown, DE
11 March 2022